The White Flag

When Compromise Cripples the Church

David S. Steele

Rom. 11:36

Here is a passionate call from a pastor's heart, from a man widely read, who sees with great clarity the difficult situation the church now faces, with opposition without and weakness and compromise within, who believes the battle will be won by the faithful believing and by the courageous teaching and proclaiming of the Word of God.

DR. PETER JONES
Director, *TruthXchange*
Author of *The Other Worldview*, Escondido, CA

In every generation, believers are called to contend earnestly for the faith, and pastors must act as watchmen on the wall, protecting the flock from danger. David Steele does exactly that in *The White Flag*. This book is overwhelmingly biblical, meticulously thorough, and refreshingly practical. Frankly, I love books like this; books that inform the mind and stir the soul!

NATE PICKOWICZ
Pastor, *Harvest Bible Church,* Gilmanton, NH
Author of *Reviving New England* and *Why We're Protestant*

Dr. David Steele exposes a clear and present danger threatening our churches. This is a biblical, bold, urgent call-to-arms reminding us that our Commander-in-Chief has entrusted to us a "Precious Treasure" that must be protected as well as proclaimed.

WAYNE PICKENS
Senior pastor, *Homestead Country Gathering*, La Grande, OR

David Steele is a champion for the truth of God's word. *The White Flag* not only exposes the destructive enemy of doctrinal compromise that threatens the contemporary church; it inspires godly courage in all believers to stand firm in defending the truth of Scripture no matter the cost. Read this excellent book to be blessed and emboldened by its timely message.

STEVE BALVANZ
Senior pastor, *Spring Creek Bible Church*, Bellingham, WA

A scholar with a shepherd's heart, Dr. David Steele guides the reader through the waters of compromise. Desiring to see the church pure and sound in doctrine, he pours out his heart with the call to be alert, for the "wolves are growling at the gate." Dr. Steele's book is saturated with Scripture and seasoned by his own pastoral experience. A must-read for anyone who loves the church.

BRYAN PICHURA
Associate pastor, *Valley Heights Community Church*, BC Canada

We are living in a day when not only is truth under attack, it is belittled, and dismissed. Our popular culture continues to churn out a message through the mainstream media that we can be all that we can be if only we will succumb to its message regarding gender roles, abortion, humanity, the climate, and more. Even as secular humanism continues to rise in our day, the Lord continues to raise up voices that challenge the status quo by calling Christians to remain faithful to biblical orthodoxy. One of these voices is Dr. David Steele. In his latest book, *The White Flag: When Compromise Cripples the Church*, Steele calls his readers to stand firm not in their own might, nor in their own righteousness, but in the righteousness of Christ. Along the way, he not only identifies the problem but points to the cure, Jesus Christ. Steele's wise and biblical counsel will help new and seasoned Christians to navigate the shifting sands of compromise by buttressing themselves in the ancient paths of sound biblical orthodoxy. *The White Flag* is a welcome addition to the calls to reformation, revival, and renewal in the church. It not only diagnoses the problem, it lays out a biblical-theological vision grounded in the gospel that will help every Christian navigate the way forward in our hedonistic, humanistic post-Christian culture to the glory of God.

DAVE JENKINS
Executive Director, *Servants of Grace Ministries*
Executive Editor, *Theology of Life Magazine*
Host, *Equipping You in Grace Podcast*

ISBN: 9781082412196

Cover design: Stephen Melniszyn, Stephen Melniszyn Designs

Interior layout: John Manning

To Dr. David P. Craig

*For your single-minded devotion to the cause of truth,
unyielding commitment to Scripture, unwavering devotion to
the flock of God, and passion to proclaim the doctrines of grace
to the nations. The white flag has never come unfurled in the
churches you've pastored, and by God's grace it never will!*

CONTENTS

Foreword

Peacetime Christianity does not exist. Not yet anyway. Not as long as we wage war with the world, the flesh, and the devil. Until Jesus comes back, the battle rages and there are no days off.

Not everyone sees it this way, of course. I remember in my first pastorate when a deacon told me that most days in his life, he spent about two minutes or less in prayer and if ever anything really serious came up he would devote a little more time to it. He and another man actually reprimanded me for suggesting that two minutes in prayer wasn't enough. It was not my desire to put a time limit on prayer, but for us to realize something that is crucial to walking with Christ: there is no such thing as peacetime Christianity.

The problem, of course, is so many live a peacetime Christianity in the midst of an all-out onslaught against the truth. Can you imagine a soldier in the midst of the fierce battle of Iwo Jima writing a letter about how great the weather was that day? Or what about a heart surgeon in the middle of a triple bypass beginning his fantasy football draft? Too many professing Christians are living casual lives almost oblivious to the compromise happening all around them, even in their own hearts, homes, and local churches.

In steps Dr. David Steele with this book, *The White Flag: When Compromise Cripples the Church*. In this book you now hold, Steele sounds the alarm on the critical state of so many local churches today which are raising the white flag of surrender to a wicked and corrupt culture instead of standing firm in truth and calling sinners to repentance and faith in Christ. It is critical that Christians today see the war for truth all around them and wake up from their slumber of capitulation. "We must," as Steele writes, "repudiate lazy, lackadaisical, passive Christianity."

As the author lays out the reality of the spirit of our present culture, the reader will be reminded that not only are there those outside the church seeking to destroy the truth, but there is arguably an even greater threat from those inside the church who intentionally or unintentionally twist the truth. Pay careful attention to Part 2 as we are shown how too many within the church are seeking to dismantle God, disregard doctrine, denigrate the work of Christ, disregard Christ's judgment, and demolish the Christian mind.

In each of these areas, too many professing believers are watering down the truth of Scripture. Sometimes this is not done intentionally but results from a chain of pragmatic choices that only hoist the white flag of compromise ever higher. And regardless of intentionality or not, there will be serious consequences for those who impugn the character of God, make light of his truth, scoff at Christ's work, neglect his coming judgment, and numb the Christian mind. The key is this: there is no neutrality! If we are not intentionally seeking to actively combat these errors, then we have placed ourselves on the wrong side of this war for truth.

When you see a medical doctor for a serious health issue you are facing, you most likely want one who will not only tell you the truth, but is also willing to go through the details of both how this happened, and what the solution is. This is exactly how Dr. Steele writes in the pages ahead. With skillful precision and an honest, yet loving bedside manner, you will be shown the truth of how the church has slipped into such a state of compromise. But you will also see the way out. Yet, I need to warn you: lowering the white flag isn't for the faint of heart. You must be willing to stand boldly upon the holy, authoritative, inspired, inerrant, and all-sufficient Scriptures. You must reaffirm your commitment to the perfect life, substitutionary death, and victorious resurrection of Christ. You must be serious about personal holiness and you must be zealous to proclaim the gospel to all people, calling them to repent of their wretched sinfulness and to flee the wrath to come by placing their faith in Christ alone as their only suitable and all-sufficient Savior.

You must understand the robustness of the Christian worldview and be willing to be a contributing soldier in the present war. You must desire to be discerning in all things and willing to graciously, yet firmly, confront those who are in moral or doctrinal error in the church. But you must also remember it's all worth it! Christ is coming soon to rule and reign with his people forever. Never forget that and in the words of Francis Schaeffer: "Keep on!"

What you will find in the pages ahead is a gospel-rich, doctrinally-sound, Christ-honoring, historically-relevant, Scripturally-saturated, intellectually stimulating, well-illustrated, and functionally useful book. Dr. Steele will step on your toes at times. He may cause you to bemoan the age in which we live. But you will be emboldened to strap on the sword of the Spirit and do battle against the forces of evil.

I bid thee well, oh reader! And if providence would have us meet somewhere down the line, may we both have a much greater resolve to never raise the white flag of surrender because we have been so masterfully and lovingly exhorted by our dear brother, David Steele. With that, I leave you to read this book for yourself.

Allen S. Nelson IV

Author of *From Death to Life: How Salvation Works* and *Before the Throne: Reflections on God's Holiness*
June 2019

Introduction

A soldier on the battlefield is pressed from every side. Enemy combatants surround the perimeter, and not only threaten his well-being but his very existence. This enemy is equipped with the most advanced weaponry and has been trained in the ways of modern-day warfare. This enemy is a well-seasoned opponent, skilled in the art of deception. This enemy is a ruthless opponent and will go to any length to achieve a decisive victory. The primary objective of this enemy is to capture or kill his opponent. Anything less than total victory is unacceptable.

In a similar way, Christ-followers are concealed in a foxhole and are surrounded by a vicious enemy. But this enemy is not a physical foe. This enemy is invisible. This enemy is spiritual; an unseen competitor. And this enemy is diabolical. This enemy is ruthless. And like the visible enemy described above, this combatant will go to any length to defeat, discourage, and demolish Christian infantrymen.

THE WORLD, THE FLESH, AND THE DEVIL

The Bible reveals the three-headed foe of every follower of Christ. The enemy is *the* **world**, *the* **flesh**, and *the* **devil** (1 John 2:15-17; John 8:44; Rom. 8:7). The aim of the world (*cosmos*) is to squeeze us into its ungodly mold (Rom. 12:2). We become conformed to the pattern of the world when we think like and live according to an ungodly agenda. Compromise sets in when we set aside God's holy standards and embrace the philosophy of the world. When the *cosmos* dictates our dreams, guides our goals, and informs our ideology, we will unwittingly fall prey to the worldly system.

The apostle Paul warned the believers in the city of Colossae about the diabolical schemes of the **world**. He admonished them, "See to it that no one takes you captive by philosophy and empty deceit, according to human tradition, according to the elemental spirits of the world, and not according to Christ" (Col. 2:8). The term for *captive* means "to carry off as a slave or lead away from the truth." The *captivity* that Paul has in mind is not a physical incarceration but an ideological and philosophical one. Philosophy is the love of wisdom. So philosophy in and of itself is not the problem. The warning that Paul sets forth here is specifically against worldly philosophy; an ideology which is grounded in the ideas of the *cosmos* and not according to Christ.

The **flesh** wages an unholy war against our souls. Carnal pleasures parade routinely before us and offer a smorgasbord of sinful stimulants. The flesh appeals to our built-in sinful desires and invites us to pursue a life of reckless hedonism. It seeks to lure us away from finding ultimate satisfaction in God and placing heartfelt trust in Christ. The writer of Proverbs illustrates the powerful appeal of the flesh by painting a portrait of a seductive woman who lures a man into her arms: "With much seductive speech she persuades him; with her smooth talk she compels him. All at once he follows her, as an ox goes to the slaughter, or as a stag is caught fast till an arrow pierces its liver; as a bird rushes into a snare; he does not know that it will cost him his life" (Prov. 7:21-23). Such is the unceasing, military-like activity of the flesh.

And the **devil** comes to steal, kill, and destroy (John 10:10). Indeed, he is a vicious murderer; a powerful enemy who utterly hates and repudiates the truth of God's Word (John 8:44). He is the great deceiver (Gen. 3:1-5), discourager (Rev. 12:10), and distorter. "If you are a saint," writes William Gurnall, "you do not need to fear that Satan will infiltrate your soul. God will not permit it. But the devil can and does attack along the borders of your faith."[1] If the enemy can twist our concept of God or the biblical description of man, he will gain a significant foothold and threaten the very foundation of our faith. If the devil can neutralize the distinction between genders, he achieves a victory of sizable proportions. If the enemy can convince us that role distinctions are of little value or consequence, he opens a significant offensive against the church and the family.

---

[1] William Gurnall, *The Christian in Complete Armour: Volume I* (Edinburgh: The Banner of Truth Trust, reprint 1655), 156.

The apostle Peter highlights the importance of being alert (1 Pet. 5:8). Likewise, Paul the apostle addresses the need for keen awareness on the part of spiritual soldiers and stresses the purpose of this imperative, namely—"so that we would not be outwitted by Satan; for we are not ignorant of his designs" (2 Cor. 2:11). The enemy in this spiritual battle is dominated by evil purposes, which requires us to be outfitted in our spiritual armor (Eph. 6:10-11). Paul describes the reason for this armor: "… That you may be able to stand against the schemes of the devil." The word *schemes* comes from the Greek term, *methodeis,* which means "deceit or trickery." Therefore, it is crucial that spiritual soldiers understand the methodology or schemes of the enemy.

The Word of God describes the nature of this battle in vivid terms: "For we do not wrestle against flesh and blood, but against the rulers, against the authorities, against the cosmic powers over this present darkness, against the spiritual forces of evil in the heavenly places" (Eph. 6:12). This is an ongoing battle, a fight that constantly wages war against our souls. "It is a battle for the truth," writes John MacArthur. "It is about ideas. It is a fight for the mind. It is a battle against false doctrines, evil ideologies, and wrong beliefs. It is a war for *truth.*"[2] This battle requires constant vigilance, attention to God's Word, and reliance on the Holy Spirit.

In this spiritual battle, we wage a holy war, as followers of Jesus Christ. Therefore, we "abstain from the passions of the flesh" (1 Pet. 2:11). To be sure, this is a different kind of war altogether. Scripture teaches us that this war is not conventional: "For though we walk in the flesh, we are not waging war according to the flesh. For the weapons of our warfare are not of the flesh but have divine power to destroy strongholds" (2 Cor. 10:3-4). Indeed, we wage an entirely different kind of war. In this battle, we are granted divine power to topple our enemy.

Paul unveils our divine strategy in this war: "We destroy arguments and every lofty opinion raised against the knowledge of God, and take every thought captive to obey Christ" (2 Cor. 10:5). Two things, in particular, need to be destroyed or demolished. First, *arguments* refer to any reasoning that is hostile to the Christian faith or promotes a belief system that is opposed to biblical Christianity.

[2] John F. MacArthur, *The Truth War: Fighting for Certainty in an Age of Deception* (Nashville: Thomas Nelson, 2007), 32.

Second, *lofty opinion* refers to an elevated structure or barrier. That is, our responsibility involves demolishing any ideology that is not consistent with the Christian worldview. These lofty opinions are to be confronted directly and toppled with spiritual authority.

We are also called upon to *take every thought captive to obey Christ*. In other words, there must be a daily incarceration. Everything that passes through our minds must come into complete submission to the lordship of our sovereign King. In his timely volume, *The Lordship of Christ*, Vern Poythress adds, "Jesus, is therefore, worthy of absolute allegiance ... We are obliged to accept the authority of Christ because he is God and is Lord of all."[3] Every thought, every desire, every affection, and every intention must be taken captive to Christ.

Scripture provides marching orders as we engage in this new kind of war: "Finally, be strong in the Lord in the strength of his might. Put on the whole armor of God, that you may be able to stand against the schemes of the devil" (Eph. 6:1-2). The apostle Paul repeats this imperative in verse 13. He instructs us to "take up the whole armor of God, that you may be able to withstand in the evil day, and having done all, to stand firm." We are admonished to put on the belt of truth, the shield of faith, and the helmet of salvation. Additionally, we are to utilize the sword of the Spirit and pray at all times in the Spirit (Eph. 6:14-19).

Scripture challenges us to stand guard and focus intently upon gospel promises as we enter the spiritual battlefield: "Therefore, preparing your minds for action, and being sober-minded, set your hope fully on the grace that will be brought to you at the revelation of Jesus Christ" (1 Pet. 1:13). Our success, therefore, is not dependent upon self-effort or human ingenuity; our success is wholly dependent on the gospel of the Lord Jesus Christ.

So we, as soldiers in a spiritual battle, do not march onto the battlefield unaware. We have been briefed as to the nature of this battle and we embrace the critical need to "wage the good warfare" as Paul told Timothy (1 Tim. 1:18). We understand the importance of maintaining a strong faith in this godless age and maintaining a

---

[3] Vern Poythress, *The Lordship of Christ: Serving Our Savior All of the Time, in All of Life, With All of Our Heart* (Wheaton: Crossway Books, 2016), Kindle edition, Loc. 279, 379.

good conscience. And we acknowledge that some have repudiated the faith, even professing believers in the church. Paul notes that Hymenaeus and Alexander failed to fight the good fight and made "shipwreck of their faith" (1 Tim. 1:19). The sobering news of these apostates should spur us to faithfulness as we strive to please our Commanding Officer.

The way forward demands a careful look at the challenges we face in the church. It demands a careful evaluation of the compromise which has wormed its way into the household of faith. And the way forward demands a concrete strategy for believers who live in a godless generation.

A NEW WAY OF LOOKING AT TRUTH

In 1968, Francis Schaeffer made a startling claim. He argued that the way people perceived truth was in the midst of a seismic shift; that is, the way people viewed truth was being fundamentally altered:

> *The present chasm between the generations has been brought about almost entirely by a change in the concept of truth … The tragedy of our situation today is that men and women are being fundamentally affected by the new way of looking at truth, and yet they have never even analyzed the drift which has taken place.*[4]

He continued, "So this change in the concept of the way we come to knowledge and truth is the most crucial problem, as I understand it, facing Christianity today."[5]

Schaeffer maintained that the notion of absolute truth was on the decline, which would ultimately lead to a system dominated and decimated by humanism. In this humanistic system, man is the sole integration point, which renders him as the *only* source of meaning, knowledge, and value. Schaeffer urged Christ-followers to resist this pagan approach to truth with all their might.

---

[4] Francis A. Schaeffer, *The Complete Works of Francis A. Schaeffer: A Christian Worldview, Volume One, A Christian View of Philosophy* (Wheaton: Crossway Books, 1968), 5.
[5] Ibid, 6.

Schaeffer's warning to the church was stern and direct: "So the Christian must resist the spirit of the world in the form it takes in his own generation. If he does not do this, he is not resisting the spirit of the world at all."[6] This worldview would lead to "the lack of absolutes and antithesis, leading to pragmatic relativism."[7] This new worldview would begin to eclipse the Christian understanding of life, meaning, morality, and truth.

Over fifty years have passed and Schaeffer's startling claim concerning the way people perceive truth has taken a tragic turn for the worse. The "new way" of looking at truth can be compared to a great serpent patiently waiting for the chance to squeeze the life out of its victim. This merciless beast slowly suffocates its prey until it remains cold and lifeless.

Yet, despite the warnings of Schaeffer and others, the church stands passively while the epistemological shift continues to take shape. The serpent squeezes with all its might and tragically, the church has no idea she is being strangled to death!

This diabolical way of viewing truth reigns supreme on the world stage. Relativism is the norm. Exclusive truth claims are routinely discarded. Absolute propositions are scorned. And any Christian who dares to set forth a dogmatic truth claim is sure to be laughed out of the room. Tragically, Christ-followers who propose statements of absolute truth are seldom welcome at the table in postmodern culture. This culture, which promotes a radical style of tolerance can only *tolerate* so much — and anything that sounds exclusive or authoritative is immediately and aggressively discarded into the ash heap.

But the "new way" of looking at truth not only rules in the marketplace of ideas; it has also invaded the church. An illustration will help demonstrate the seriousness of this problem: Imagine a grade school student who passionately promotes the notion that two plus two equals fifteen. Imagine a high school student who argues that Einstein's theory of relativity is a farce. Or consider a college student who repudiates the assassination of Abraham Lincoln or John F. Kennedy. In each of these illustrations, the respective teachers

---

[6] Ibid, 11.
[7] Ibid.

would strike down the erroneous propositions. Each student would be guided in the way of truth, as we should expect. Such is the path of a quality education and rationality.

Now imagine three individuals who make truth claims in the local church. First, consider a Christ-follower who holds that Scripture is inerrant, infallible, authoritative, and God-breathed. Imagine an elder who affirms that every unbeliever will face the almighty wrath of God at the final judgment. And finally, imagine a pastor who teaches that God predestines specific individuals before the foundation of the world, apart from foreseen faith.

We have entered an age where each of the examples cited above are likely to receive criticism for their dogmatic assertions at best and be condemned as divisive at worst. Truth that is presented with boldness is routinely belittled and marginalized in many churches. Christians who announce the unvarnished truth of God's Word are cast aside, criticized, and ultimately condemned.

Simply put, our postmodern culture will not tolerate Christ-followers who make dogmatic statements of propositional truth without paying a terrible price. And too often, professing Christians themselves embrace the lie of relativism. Peter Kreeft demonstrates the mindset of such a person: "Their minds know the truth, but their hearts don't love it, don't submit to it, so they give it up, they exchange it for a lie; the comfortable relativistic lie that they don't have to submit."[8] They become autonomous and subtly disregard the Word of God and his sovereign authority over them.

So, the church faces a choice in the days ahead: Will we stand strong and maintain our allegiance to Scripture and the timeless truths of the gospel? Or will we capitulate and compromise? Will we concede to worldly philosophy and the twisted ideas of men? Will we raise the *white flag* and surrender to the world? Unfortunately, in many cases, we find the church capitulating to culture and compromising biblical standards. Too often, the church is conceding to error. The church in large measure is failing to confront the spirit of the age. And in the final analysis, the church has essentially lost her nerve.

---

[8] Peter Kreeft, *A Refutation of Moral Relativism* (San Francisco: Ignatius Press, 1999), 24.

Much of the compromise in the church has gone undetected. David Randall tells a story about a home which was ravaged by an unknown enemy:

An Australian home-owner came home one day to find that his house had collapsed; all that was left was a pile of dust and rubble. It transpired that, unbeknown to him, white ants have been eating away at the foundations and supporting timbers of the house for years. Everything had continued to look normal on the outside, but internally the house was being gradually consumed, until one day it crashed to the ground - destroyed by the tiny insects.[9]

Tragically, the contemporary church finds herself in a similar predicament. The foundations are slowly eroding while the "white ants" steadily consume the infrastructure of the church. Os Guinness acknowledges the tragic condition of the church and urges us to repent and obey:

It is surely time for some Christians to tremble when we read and hear the casual twisting and discarding of Scripture by those who still claim to be faithful. There is a rottenness in the church that must be addressed. Christians too need to return and stand humbly and obediently with all their fellow believers before the lordship and authority of Jesus Pantocrator, ruler, sustainer and judge of all the world.[10]

In a similar way, the psalmist laments, "If the foundations are destroyed, what can the righteous do?" (Ps. 11:3). And here is the rub: Very few people seem to care. We are simply content to gaze upon the crumbling foundations and witness the devastating effects of compromise. "There are too many Christians weary of taking a stand because they are so wary of repeating the mistakes of the past. They have become 'whatever' people, those who hedge their bets

---

[9] *Barnabas Aid,* May/June 2007, 2. Cited by David Randall, *A Sad Departure* (Carlisle: The Banner of Truth Trust, 2015), 129.

[10] Os Guinness, *Impossible People: Christian Courage and the Struggle for the Soul of Civilization* (Downers Grove: InterVarsity Press, 2016), Kindle edition, Loc. 1460.

and watch from the sidelines to see who will win the contest on the Mount Carmels of our day."[11] The bitter result is a compromised faith that succumbs to the whims of postmodernity.

It is as if the church has hoisted a *white flag* into the air and surrendered to the spirit of the age. Stephen E. Ambrose describes the paralyzing effects of surrender on soldiers who give up in battle:

> *One of the most dangerous moments in combat in Europe in World War II came the instant a man decided he was no longer willing or able to continue combat. He threw down his weapon and raised his hands, or showed a white flag ... and thus exposed himself to an armed enemy soldier he had been trying to kill a moment before ... His chances of getting shot were high. They stayed high until he was safely in the rear of the POW cage.*[12]

When Christ-followers compromise their biblical values and succumb to the spirit of the age, they are rendered immobile like the fallen soldier described above. A crippling effect sets in when convictions are surrendered and godly standards are set aside. Such a "soldier" becomes marginalized and ineffective. This "soldier" brings reproach on the church, dishonors the church, and fails to glorify the living God.

The White Flag: When Compromise Cripples the Church diagnoses the current condition of the church and offers biblical encouragement for marching forward in a way that honors and glorifies the Lord. Part One will present the *challenge* the church faces. Part Two will examine some of the most troubling aspects of the *compromised* church. And Part Three will chart a path forward and spell out a concrete strategy, or *a call to the church*. May God grant much grace as we strive to make progress for the good of the church and for his glory alone.

---

[11] Ibid, Loc. 1472.

[12] Stephen E. Ambrose, *Citizen Soldiers* (New York: Simon and Schuster, 1996), 351.

PART ONE:

THE CHALLENGED CHURCH

"Whoever marries the spirit of this age, will find himself a widower in the next."

WILLIAM RALPH INGE

1

Confronting the Spirit of the Age

"But false prophets also arose among the people, just as there will be false teachers among you, who will secretly bring in destructive heresies, even denying the Master who bought them, bringing upon themselves swift destruction. And many will follow their sensuality, and because of them the way of truth will be blasphemed. And in their greed they will exploit you with false words. Their condemnation from long ago is not idle, and their destruction is not asleep."

2 PETER 2:1-3

The German word *zeitgeist* nicely captures what we face in the contemporary church. The word means "spirit of the age." This is precisely what Scripture calls us to confront, namely, the worldly system that militates against God's Word and the Christian worldview. The *zeitgeist* is deeply entrenched in our cultural milieu. It is carefully spliced into popular books and movies. It has strangled our courtrooms. It is embedded in our system of public education. Simply put, the *zeitgeist* has, for the most part, captured the American mind.

Confronting the *zeitgeist* demands a positive identification. Dean Inge remarks, "He who marries the spirit of the age soon finds himself a widower."[13] Therefore, we must learn to properly identify people who are in step with the spirit of the age.

IDENTIFYING FALSE PROPHETS

In the first century, the apostle Peter identified a group of people he referred to as "false prophets." This cadre of conspirators was on a mission and had a definite sense of purpose. Their mission continues to unfold as false prophets and false teachers emerge before our very eyes. These truth twisters remain deeply committed to destroying the doctrinal standards of Scripture. Their ultimate aim is to lay the truth of Scripture to rest and forever stifle the influence of the saints.

A false prophet is a pseudo-prophet. This person is a phony—a sham. This con artist teaches damning doctrine in the name of God. The false prophet is a counterfeiter. Like a criminal who attempts to pass a bogus bill, the false prophet advances pirated ideas that look good on the surface but are erroneous. Some of these false prophets wear robes; others don a coat and tie. You see them in airports; you see them at your front door; you see them riding on bicycles in pairs. You see them on television—you even see them on Christian television. But the fact remains—false prophets and false teachers cannot stay in the shadows forever. They eventually come bursting into the light of day and foist their diabolical doctrine on unsuspecting minds and naïve hearts.

The modus operandi of these false prophets is clearly set forth in Scripture. Their strategy is plain and their methodology is consistent from age to age. The apostle Peter notes several strands of DNA that make up these doctrine distorters.

First, *false prophets are determined.* Peter says that false teachers "arose among the people ..." (2 Pet. 2:1a). The single-minded efforts of false teachers are nothing new—but what is especially alarming is that they actually made their ascent in the church. Indeed, as the apostle John acknowledges, "for many false prophets have gone out into the world" (1 John 4:1b).

Peter makes it clear that their strategy involved "secrecy." Their persistent efforts to promote false doctrine under fabricated pretense

---

[13] Cited in Os Guinness, *The Last Christian on Earth: Uncover the Enemy's Plot to Undermine the Church* (Grand Rapids: Baker Books), 200.

is covert theological activity. This is a cloak-and-dagger mission. What usually begins underground eventually makes its way into the leadership structure of the unsuspecting church. Scripture consistently identifies this trend among the deceived and among the deceptive. Jude 4a says, "For certain people have crept in unnoticed who long ago were designated for this condemnation." 2 Corinthians 11:13 says, "For such men are false apostles, deceitful workmen, disguising themselves as apostles of Christ." And Paul adds the following plea to the Ephesian elders: "I know that after my departure fierce wolves will come in among you, not sparing the flock; and from among your own selves will arise men speaking twisted things, to draw away the disciples after them" (Acts 20:29–30).

Second, *false prophets bring destruction*. Peter specifically charges these false teachers with bringing "destructive heresies." The apostle Paul identifies the source of these heresies: "Now the Spirit expressly says that in later times some will depart from the faith by devoting themselves to deceitful spirits and teachings of demons..." (1 Tim. 4:1). Jesus indicates that these false teachers will "arise and lead many astray" (Matt. 24:11).

Of course, we are not talking about doctrinal matters on which we can agree to disagree on. We are not talking about open-handed, disputable matters. We are not referring to debatable matters like the mode of baptism, the timing of the return of Christ, or the specifics of the millennial reign of Christ.[14] Rather, we are talking about teaching which is diametrically opposed to Scripture—teaching that is, by definition, destructive in nature. This kind of teaching is heretical. Irenaeus observes, "Error, indeed, is never set forth in its naked deformity, lest, being thus exposed, it should at once be detected. But it is craftily decked out in an attractive dress, so as, by its outward form, to make it appear to the inexperienced (ridiculous as the expression may seem) more true than truth itself."[15]

Third, *false prophets deny the truth about Jesus*. The apostle Peter notes, "But false prophets also arose among the people, just as there

---

[14] This is not to suggest that these matters are unimportant. But these debatable matters should not be a test for orthodoxy.

[15] Iranaeus, Cited in Harold O.J. Brown, *Heresies: Heresy and Orthodoxy in the History of the Church* (Peabody: Hendrickson Publishers, 1984), 6.

will be false teachers among you, who will secretly bring in destructive heresies, even denying the Master who bought them, bringing upon themselves swift destruction" (2 Pet. 2:1). This remark reminds us of an important principle, namely—false teachers are not only identified by what they affirm, they are also identified by who they deny, in this case, the person and work of the Lord Jesus Christ. The apostle John stresses this fundamental reality: Anyone who denies that Jesus is from God is the spirit of the antichrist (1 John 4:3).

Fourth, *false prophets desecrate the truth of God's Word.* The apostle Peter adds, "And many will follow their sensuality, and because of them the way of truth will be blasphemed" (2 Pet. 2:2). Jude recognizes this same reality: "For certain people have crept in unnoticed who long ago were designated for this condemnation, ungodly people, who pervert the grace of our God into sensuality and deny our only Master and Lord, Jesus Christ" (Jude 4). These truth robbers pervert the grace of God by adding requirements to the gospel. They subvert the grace of God by muddying the waters of free grace. And when grace is polluted, they not only desecrate the truth of God's Word—they deny Jesus Christ.

Fifth, *false prophets distract people from hearing the truth of Scripture.* The apostle Peter writes, "And in their greed they will exploit you …" (2 Pet. 2:3). If false prophets can distract or divert the attention of the listener, he or she will have gained a significant inroad into the lives of the unsuspecting. False teachers focus on doctrinal hobby-horses and lead people away from the pure milk of the Word. As the serpent distracted Eve, so too will false teachers deceive people and lead them astray (2 Cor. 11:3).

Sixth, *false prophets deceive people.* How does this deception take place? How do they do it? Peter says, " … They will exploit you with false words" (v. 3). The term *exploit* comes from the business world. It means "to deceive for personal gain." Their agenda, then, is a matter of deception. False prophets will use deceitful ideology to lure gullible people into their tangled web of lies.

Seventh, *false prophets are destined for damnation.* Scripture could not be any clearer on this matter. False prophets have a final destination; they are destined for judgment. Peter says, "Their condemnation from long ago is not idle, and their destruction is not asleep" (2 Pet. 2:3). Peter saw no hope for these apostates; their doom was sealed. His attitude was different from that of "tolerant" religious people today who say, "Well, they may not agree with us, but there are many roads to heaven." [16]

It should come as no surprise, then, when false prophets and false teachers emerge from the shadows. We do not say, "If false teachers come." We say, "When false teachers come." The fact is this: We will always have false teachers to contend with until Jesus returns. One day, Jesus will make all things new but until that day, we will be forced to deal with their evil influence. These charlatans will infiltrate our neighborhoods. They will influence the workplace. You will see them on television. You will read about them in books. Sometimes, as we have seen—they will make their way into the local church. They may even worm their way into the upper levels of leadership.

Gresham Machen fought strenuously on the front lines against the false prophets in the middle of the 20th century. Machen identifies the primary opponent of the day: "The chief modern rival of Christianity is 'liberalism.' An examination of the teachings of liberalism in comparison with those of Christianity will show that at every point the two movements are in direct opposition." [17] With these false teachers in our sights, let us examine their condition.

THE CONDITION OF FALSE PROPHETS

In the first century, Jude most likely wrote about the preliminary stages of Gnosticism which would strike the church in a matter of years. [18] The Gnostics taught that matter was evil and spirit was good. They maintained that since the flesh was not created by God, it was proper to succumb to sinful desires. Jude notes three characteristics of these false prophets, all of which appear in Jude 1:4.

---

[16] Wiersbe, W. W. (1996). The Bible exposition commentary (Vol. 2, 448). Wheaton, IL: Victor Books.

[17] J. Gresham Machen, *Christianity and Liberalism* (Grand Rapids: Eerdmans, 1923), 1-2.

[18] The apostle John battled the Gnostic heresy in his letters written in approximately A.D. 90-95, almost twenty-five years after Jude wrote his epistle.

First, *they were ungodly*. The Greek term for *ungodly* describes a person who has repudiated God. This person does not love God, worship God, or have any desire to serve him. This is a description of an irreverent person. Paul expands his definition of the ungodly in 1 Timothy 1:9-10 by noting that they are among the "murderers, the sexually immoral, men who practice homosexuality, enslavers, liars, perjurers, and whatever else is contrary to sound doctrine." Peter utilizes the same word for the ungodly in 2 Peter 3:7 which places them in a position of being judged eternally for their sin.

Second, *they pervert the grace of God.* Jude defines this perversion in narrow terms. He says they "pervert the grace of our God into sensuality." The term *pervert* describes a person who changes from one state to another. It means to "abandon or desert someone." It means "to make an exchange, in this case, from the grace of God into a condition of sensuality (*aselgeia*)." The sensuality that Jude has in mind can be translated as "debauchery, lewdness or licentiousness." The person who perverts the grace of God into sensuality is completely unrestrained. They do as they please, when they please, and passionately pursue a self-centered agenda. They have a reckless disregard for the Word of God and the ways of God. These false teachers pervert the grace of God.

Third, *they deny Jesus Christ. Deny (arneomai)* means "to verbally renounce knowledge or a relationship." The term means "a refusal to submit to or adhere to the commands of another, in this case, the Lord Jesus Christ." There is no ambiguity there. False teachers are completely unwilling to adhere to or consent to the teaching of Jesus.

False teachers *deny the deity of Christ.* The apostle John warns us about the prospect of such a person and sets forth clear guidelines for recognizing this theological poser:

> *Beloved, do not believe every spirit, but test the spirits to see whether they are from God, for many false prophets have gone out into the world. By this you know the Spirit of God: every spirit that confesses that Jesus Christ has come in the flesh is from God, and every spirit that does not confess Jesus is not from God. This is the spirit of the antichrist, which you heard was coming and now is in the world already (1 John 4:1–3).*

John paints a clear portrait of a person who may look good and sound good, but denies that Jesus is from God. Such a person "is the spirit of the antichrist."

Next, false teachers *deny the substitutionary work of Christ on the cross*. In recent days, it has become fashionable for teachers and preachers to tinker with the atoning work of Christ. In the most extreme cases, we find these teachers repudiating the substitutionary work of Christ, which is tantamount to theological treason.

And false teachers *promote a works-based system of salvation*. An example of this pernicious form of false teaching is found in the theological framework of the Judaizers. The apostle Paul refers to them as "false brothers" (*pseudàdelphos*) in Galatians 2:4. The Greek term refers to a person who pretends to be a member of a group. Paul includes "false brothers" among the list of dangerous people in his letter to the Corinthians (2 Cor. 11:22-27). Like the false teachers that Jude addressed, these heretics secretly slipped into the local church. These stealthy hoodlums flew under the radar and used deceptive means to accomplish their diabolical mission.

Galatians 2:4-5 describes the essence of their mission: "Yet because of false brothers secretly brought in—who slipped in to spy out our freedom that we have in Christ Jesus, so that they might bring us into slavery— to them we did not yield in submission even for a moment, so that the truth of the gospel might be preserved for you." These false teachers were requiring Gentile Christ-followers to get circumcised. Such a practice would render the believer a slave to his former unconverted way of life.

Whenever we add a condition to grace, we become enslaved; we revert to our old way of living. Whenever we add a condition to the gracious provision of the gospel, we ultimately abandon the gospel, which is shorthand for abandoning Christ. "Paul saw very clearly that the difference between the Judaizers and himself was the difference between two entirely distinct types of religion," writes J. Gresham Machen. "It was the difference between a religion of merit and a religion of grace. If Christ provides only a part of our salvation, leaving us to provide the rest, then we are still hopeless under the load of sin."[19] At any rate, false teachers famously parade their works-based righteousness for the world to see and demand Christ-followers to do the same.

WOLVES AT THE GATE

These are the prophets that Scripture warns us about—false prophets, ungodly hucksters who pervert the grace of God and deny the person and work of the Lord Jesus Christ. The arrival of these ferocious wolves should come as no surprise to the student of God's Word. For Paul warned, "I know that after my departure fierce wolves will come in among you, not sparing the flock; and from among your own selves will arise men speaking twisted things, to draw away the disciples after them" (Acts 20:29-30). Yet the lies of the devil are deceitful and filled with cunning strategy. Michael Horton notes, "... Satan knows from experience that sowing heresy and schism is far more effective. While the blood of the martyrs is the seed of the church, the assimilation of the church to the world silences the witness."[20]

The lies and false teaching perpetrated by these wolves will be ongoing and will require vigilance on the part of faithful followers of Christ. Failure to confront this kind of error will lead to the tragic departure of some people who are deceived and lured away by these malicious enemies of the faith.

The wolves at the gate must be confronted directly and decisively. They must be rebuked and admonished. Yet, what we find in the postmodern church is something completely different. Instead of confrontation, the church capitulates. Instead of drawing the line in the sand, the church deviates from the truth. Instead of boldly addressing the doctrinal error of these pandering prophets, they are given a wide range of latitude in the church. In order for churches to respond properly to these theological wolves, we must learn to discern the zeitgeist. We must be willing to confront the spirit of the age. Churches who refuse to exercise biblical discernment will pay a terrible price.

---

[19] J. Gresham Machen, *Christianity and Liberalism*, 24.
[20] Michael Horton, *Christless Christianity: The Alternative Gospel of the American Church* (Grand Rapids: Baker Books, 2008), Kindle edition, Loc. 106.

2

Discerning the Spirit of the Age

"Beloved, do not believe every spirit, but test the spirits to see whether they are from God, for many false prophets have gone out into the world. By this you know the Spirit of God: every spirit that confesses that Jesus Christ has come in the flesh is from God, and every spirit that does not confess Jesus is not from God. This is the spirit of the antichrist, which you heard was coming and now is in the world already."

1 JOHN 4:1-3

As we have observed, the postmodern zeitgeist is flourishing in the church. This seditious monster seeks to undermine and weaken the church. Its subversive activity is done in the shadows and works tirelessly to sabotage and incapacitate God's people. Done correctly, the church will not even recognize the damage or discern any noticeable difference.

Martin Luther is one of the few Christ-followers who recognized the devious and malicious nature of the zeitgeist in the 16th century. He wrote about it in his well-known work, *The Babylonian Captivity of the Church.* Os Guinness rightly identifies this weakness as a "falling for the spirit, style, and system of the age, which is also a worldliness and an unfaithfulness that both saps the strength of the church and brings it under the judgment of God."[21] Luther saw the devious ways of the zeitgeist and warned the church to flee from its

---

[21] Os Guinness, *The Last Christian on Earth: Uncover the Enemy's Plot to Undermine the Church*, 10.

diabolical ways: "Beware, therefore, that the external pomp of works and the deceits of man-made ordinances do not deceive you, lest you wrong the divine truth and your faith." [22] Tragically, many failed to heed his counsel. The same holds true in our generation.

Luther was quick to identify the *spirit of the age* during the formative days of the Reformation: "See how far the glory of the church has departed! The whole earth is filled with priests, bishops, cardinals, and clergy; yet not one of them preaches so far as his official duty is concerned, unless he is called to do so by a different call over and above his sacramental ordination."[23] The relentless reformer fulfilled his biblical duty and discerned the spirit of the age.[24] The church benefited greatly from his godly wisdom then and continues to reap the benefits in the present day.

The apostle John describes our battle-ready position. He establishes two benchmarks which will enable us to discern the spirit of the age.

DISTINGUISHING BETWEEN GOOD AND EVIL

John the apostle sets forth the first of two imperatives—both appearing in the first verse of Chapter 4: "Beloved, do not believe every spirit, but test the spirits to see whether they are from God, for many false prophets have gone out into the world" (1 John 4:1).

The first imperative involves distinguishing between good and evil and may be stated as follows: *Do not believe everything you hear.* Notice the keywords—*do not believe.* The Greek term translated *believe* means "to render a statement as true; to be persuaded in the truthfulness of something"—in this case, the spirit of error.

Here is the reality: we distinguish each and every day. Whenever we pull up to a stoplight, we distinguish between red and green. When we eat dinner, we distinguish between meat and potatoes, between vegetables and dessert. When we go to the grocery store, we

---

[22] Martin Luther, The Babylonian Captivity of the Church, Cited in *Three Treatises* (Fortress Press, 1943), Kindle edition, Loc. 1937.

[23] Ibid, Loc. 2617.

[24] See David S. Steele, *Bold Reformer: Celebrating the Gospel-Centered Convictions of Martin Luther* (Brenham: Lucid Books, 2016).

distinguish between brands. Some choose name brands; some opt for generic. When we search for a hotel to lodge in for summer vacation, we distinguish the affordable from the expensive. When our children bring home their report cards, we distinguish between an A-plus and a C-minus. In the Christian life, we must distinguish between good ideas and evil ideas. We distinguish the beautiful from the profane. Whenever someone sets forth a worldview or advances some sort of ideology, we must evaluate those ideas through the lens of sacred Scripture.

"Philosophy forces us to think foundationally," writes R.C. Sproul.[25] "Foundational thinking lays bare all of our assumptions so that we may discover those assumptions that are false and often lethal."[26] The Bible calls us to distinguish between good and evil ideology for this reason: ideas have consequences. For example, in 1859 a book was published—a book that would gain quick notoriety and influence many generations to come. When Charles Darwin published *The Origin of Species*, he threw down the gauntlet and cast a radical vision: a naturalistic worldview which has gained the ascendency in most universities and continues to compete for the hearts and minds of people to this day. Darwin's ideas, however, have massive consequences. His worldview influences the way we view ourselves, our purpose in the world, and our final destiny.

Friedrich Engels, the co-author of *The Communist Manifesto* (1863) writes, "In our evolutionary conception of the universe, there is absolutely no room for either a Creator or a Ruler."[27] The Creator is obsolete, then, and man is rendered as the final arbiter of truth. Engels' worldview is a direct reflection of the ideology that Darwin promoted in *The Origin of Species*. Clearly, then, ideas have far-reaching consequences that impact our view of God, authority, man, eternity and our final destiny.

Or consider the example of Margaret Sanger, the founder of *Planned Parenthood*. Sanger was a proponent of Eugenics—defined as the "self-direction of human evolution," a notion which is similar

---

[25] R.C. Sproul, *The Consequences of Ideas* (Wheaton: Crossway Books, 2000), 9.

[26] Ibid, 11.

[27] Friedrich Engels, *Socialism, Utopian, and Scientific* (Chicago: Charles H. Kerry and Company, 1910), 19.

to Darwin's so-called survival of the fittest. Like Marx and Engels, Sanger was influenced by the worldview Darwin promoted. Faye Wattleton, who served as President of *Planned Parenthood* from 1978 to 1992 writes, "We are not going to be an organization promoting celibacy or chastity."[28] These are only a few examples of how the ideology of the world is impacting our lives.

Once again, this serves as a sort of wake-up call. It reminds us that ideas have grave consequences. Whenever we fail to distinguish between good and evil, we give evil a foothold and unwittingly surrender ground in the Christian race. Losing ground is always the first step to losing the war. We must, therefore, follow the apostle John's lead—we must distinguish between good and evil.

DISCERNING TRUTH FROM ERROR

The second benchmark the Apostle John establishes is also found in 1 John 4:1. "Beloved, do not believe every spirit, but test the spirits to see whether they are from God, for many false prophets have gone out into the world." Wolves frequently mix truth with error. Ravi Zacharias warns, "When you mix falsehood with truth, you create a more destructive lie."[29] All the more reason to discern truth from error!

The second imperative is a logical extension of the first one: *Test everything you see and hear.* John's directive means "to determine the worthiness of something." In this case, we *test* the spirits to see whether they are from God. Paul uses the same word in 1 Thessalonians 5:21. He writes, "... but *test* everything; hold fast what is good." John R.W. Stott observes, "So behind every prophet is a spirit, and behind every spirit either God or the devil. Before we can trust any spirits, we must test them."[30]

Tim Challies highlights the importance of discernment in the Christian life: "Discernment is the skill of understanding and applying God's Word with the purpose of separating truth from error and

[28] Los Angeles Times, October 17, 1986
[29] Ravi Zacharias, *The Lotus and the Cross: Jesus Talks with Buddha* (Colorado Springs: Multnomah, 2012), Kindle edition, Loc. 266.
[30] John R.W. Stott, *Tyndale New Testament Commentaries: The Letters of John* (Downers Grove: IVP Academic, 1988), 153.

right from wrong."[31] King Solomon presents a request to God that reflects a heart for biblical discernment:

> *Give your servant therefore an understanding mind to govern your people, that I may discern between good and evil, for who is able to govern this your great people? (1 Kings 3:9).*

> *And God said to him, "Because you have asked this, and have not asked for yourself long life or riches or the life of your enemies, but have asked for yourself understanding to discern what is right ... " (1 Kings 3:11).*

We are constantly making judgments. We discern every day. For example, a quarterback discerns as he steps up to the line of scrimmage. He carefully evaluates his opponent and makes the necessary adjustments in his strategy before the ball is snapped. A sailor discerns as he meticulously evaluates the weather patterns and makes the necessary adjustments to his travels plans. And a physician discerns as she evaluates the health of her patients and monitors their vital signs.

DISCERNMENT IN THE CHRISTIAN LIFE

Exercising biblical discernment is the special responsibility of every Christ-follower. It is not a privilege for the educated elite or the ministerial "professionals." While some are no doubt blessed with the spiritual gift of discernment, Scripture is clear that each of us must be discerning as we engage with the surrounding culture. Notice several observations that concern the mandate before us to discern:

First, *discernment is a learned skill.* Learning to discern is a skill that takes practice. Developing discernment takes time, and needs to be nurtured on a daily basis. Colossians 2:8 admonishes believers, "See to it that no one takes you captive by philosophy and empty deceit, according to human tradition, according to the elemental spirits of the world, and not according to Christ." The Greek term, *blepō* is translated, "see to it" here and involves careful discernment. This im-

---

[31] Tim Challies, *The Discipline of Spiritual Discernment* (Wheaton: Crossway Books, 2008), 61.

perative means to "weigh carefully" or "examine something." There is an urgency attached to this command. It would be like crossing the piranha-infested Amazon River. The river guide would cry out, "*Watch out (blepō)*—keep your hands out of the water!"

The Bible utilizes the term *blepō* in several passages:

> *And Jesus answered them, 'Watch out' (blepō) that no one deceives you (Matt. 24:4, NIV).*

> *And Jesus began to say to them, 'See (blepō) that no one leads you astray' (Mark 13:5).*

> *And he cautioned them, saying, 'Watch out; beware (blepō) of the leaven of the Pharisees and the leaven of Herod' (Mark 8:15).*

Scripture warns us about the possibility of falling prey to spiritual deception. It warns us to beware of the subtle influences of culture that threaten to undermine the church and do violence to our souls. The challenge before each Christ-follower, then, is to nurture the skill of discernment. We must view everything through a biblical filter—all to the glory of God. Nothing is to escape our watchful eye.

Second, *discernment takes discipline*. We must stand our ground; we must be alert; we must repudiate lazy, lackadaisical, passive Christianity. Paul reminds us to discipline ourselves for the purpose of godliness (1 Tim. 4:7). There is an intentional link, then, between discernment and discipline. That is to say, disciplined Christ-followers are discerning. Undisciplined people are both undiscerning and disobedient.

An important aspect of developing discipline is to be constantly aware of our surroundings. Our challenge is to constantly monitor the world in which we live. Russell Moore highlights the importance of this special mindset: "The world system around us, the cultural matrix we inhabit, is alien to the kingdom of God—with different priorities, different strategies, and a different vision of the future. If we don't see that we are walking a narrow and counterintuitive road, we will have nothing distinctive to say because we will have forgotten who we are."[32] Such vigilance not only preserves our salty influence

---

[32] Russell Moore, *Onward: Engaging the Culture Without Losing the Gospel* (Nashville:

in culture, it prevents a pitiful marginalization which is so common among Christians.

Third, *discernment is about making judgments.* Making a judgment call on anything in our culture is an automatic source of controversy. The postmodern mind recoils against authority; it resists the notion of distinguishing between truth and error. But Scripture calls us to judge in this respect. The Greek word, *diakronō* (1 Cor. 11:29) means "to separate or judge." The word *kritikós* (Heb. 4:12) means "able to judge." And *ànakrínō* means "to question, judge, or carefully examine." So making judgments, much to the chagrin of the world, is a normal part of the Christian life.

Fourth, *being a person of discernment makes its final appeal to the Word of God.* Again, this is vexing to the postmodern mind because it appeals to a higher authority, which is to suggest that one is holding to an absolute standard, namely—absolute truth. Christians who cling, then, to the authoritative Word of God should be prepared for unrelenting backlash and persecution.

Next, *being a person of discernment assumes there is a right way and a wrong way.* The Greek word, *dokimádzō* means "to prove or examine; to discern, distinguish, or approve." The term describes something that demonstrates the worthiness of something. Paul utilizes this term in several passages:

> *Do not be conformed to this world, but be transformed by the renewal of your mind, that by testing you may* **discern** *(dokimádzō) what is the will of God, what is good and acceptable and perfect (Rom. 12:2).*

> *… For the Day will disclose it, because it will be revealed by fire, and the fire will* **test** *(dokimádzō) what sort of work each one has done (1 Cor. 3:13).*

> *Let a person* **examine** *(dokimádzō) himself, then, and so eat of the bread and drink of the cup (1 Cor. 11:28).*

Christ-followers who exercise discernment must believe and embrace the law of non-contradiction. Too many evangelicals these days

B&H Publishing, 2015), 29.

want every person to be right. Such a view is not realistic. Such a view does not accord with reality or align with the way God created the world. By definition, then, a person of discernment affirms a distinction between right and wrong.

Finally, *being a person of discernment assumes that truth is objective—and not subjective.* It implies that truth is exclusive and binds the conscience of all people. Of course, some things in life *are* subjective. I was reminded of this recently as I took my kids for an ice-cream outing. My daughter got a scoop of cappuccino in a cup. My son got vanilla soft serve on a cone—his favorite. I tried a new flavor, coconut almond bliss. Each of us enjoyed our treat, and each of us was convinced that "ours was the best." Incidentally, the coconut almond bliss *was* the best! There is no absolute standard of truth that can be applied to ice cream, baseball teams, or hamburger restaurants. But when it comes to matters of epistemology, or the nature of truth—we recognize there is an objective standard that must be ruthlessly applied.

TESTS FOR EXERCISING BIBLICAL DISCERNMENT

The apostle John supplies two specific tests for exercising biblical discernment in 1 John 4. Remember that we are called to discern truth from error. Therefore, we are primarily concerned with the ideas people put before us and the philosophy which is peddled in the marketplace of ideas.

First, *do they promote a blemished Christ?* Do they promote a view of Christ that is in alignment with the Word of God? Do they emphasize Christ's humanity and ignore, deny, or marginalize his deity? Do they emphasize Christ's deity and ignore, deny, or marginalize his humanity in any way? Do they, with the ancient Gnostics, view creation as evil and spirit as good, and as a result repudiate the humanity of Jesus Christ?

Consider the Muslim view of Christ. In a Muslim scheme, Jesus was a messenger of God, not the Son of God. In a Muslim theological framework, Jesus is *not* divine. Islam maintains that Christ did not die on the cross for sinners. Muslims agree on this fundamental premise: Jesus is not the final revelation of God. Such a view distorts the Christ of the Bible. Therefore, Islam promotes a blemished Christ.

Or consider the view promoted by the Watchtower Society. The Jehovah's Witnesses maintain that Jesus is not God in the flesh: " … The true Scriptures speak of God's Son, the Word, as a 'god.' He is 'a mighty god,' but not the Almighty God, who is Jehovah."[33] So Jehovah's Witnesses openly deny the deity of Jesus Christ.

Calvin is quick to confront anyone who does not present a biblical portrait of Christ: "Those who rob Christ of divinity or humanity either detract from his majesty and glory or obscure his goodness."[34] The apostle John responds with similar passion—for anyone who rejects the full humanity and deity of Christ is not of God. He notes, "This is the spirit of the antichrist" (v. 3).

John's second test is similar to the first, namely—*do they promote a blemished worldview?* What do they teach about God? What are their doctrinal commitments? Do they affirm the penal substitutionary atonement of Christ on the cross for sinners? Do they affirm the doctrine of eternal punishment for the unrepentant? Does God's Word bind their conscience and compel them to live under the weight of its authority? Are they using their minds for the glory of God and submitting everything to the lordship of Christ? Is their ultimate allegiance bound to the Word of God or are they tethered to the frail tassel of human autonomy?

The wolves are growling at the gate. Like the days of the first century, some of these wolves have invaded the local church. They have weaseled their way into the front doors. Like crafty snakes, they have slithered through the back door. They have wormed their way into positions of authority. They have managed to find leadership roles in influential arenas. They have secured elected positions as deacons and elders. Some of these wolves are serving as pastors. Their agenda is simple: seek and destroy. These wolves have no regard for truth. They have no love for orthodoxy. And they pay no homage to a holy God.

---

[33] *The Truth Shall Make You Free:* Brooklyn: Watchtower Bible and Tract Society, 1943), 47. Cited in Walter Martin, *Kingdom of the Cults* (Minneapolis: Bethany House Publishers, 1965), 53.

[34] John Calvin, *Institutes of the Christian Religion* (Peabody: Hendrickson, reprint 2008), 299.

Indeed, we live in the day of the challenged church. We live in a day which is marked by theological error and apostasy. We live in a day in which truth is maligned and contradiction is celebrated. While many are rightly concerned by the prospect of a terrorist attack, perhaps we should set our sights on theological terrorism, which has infiltrated the church.

Our task is to return to our first love. Peter Jones admonishes the church: "We must call all cultures and ourselves—in every generation to the rule that judges all other rules—the rule of faith, the law of true freedom, the Word of God."[35] A cursory glance across the cultural milieu reveals an unfurled *white flag*. The *white flag* has been unfurled and a diabolical deal has been struck. This flag reveals a horrifying reality, which must be addressed, namely—final surrender in the compromised church. This *white flag*, if left unchecked, will cripple the church. In Part Two, we shall turn our attention to some of the symptoms of the compromised church.

---

[35] Peter Jones, *The Other Worldview: Exposing Christianity's Greatest Threat* (Bellingham: Kirkdale Press, 2015), 6.

PART TWO

THE COMPROMISED CHURCH

"Absolutely nothing in traditional belief or practice is sacrosanct. There are no higher or central truths by which the Church will stand or fall. Heresy is orthodoxy; skepticism is faith; no paganism is too wild and no ethical practice too abnormal to be turned away from their inclusive embrace. Everything is negotiable, the kernel as well as the husk, the baby as well as the bath water."[36]

[36] Os Guinness, *The Last Christian on Earth: Uncover the Enemy's Plot to Undermine the Church*, 201.

3

Dismantling God

"An open mind, like an open mouth, does have a purpose: and that is, to close it upon something solid. Otherwise, it could end up like a city sewer, rejecting nothing."

G.K. CHESTERTON [37]

The first sign of the compromised church is a God who has been dismantled. This is the first of several signs that we will examine, signs that are an indication of spiritual weakness and apathy. All of these signs reveal the net effect of the rising *white flag,* which has been hoisted high by a church that has lost both her courage and her theological nerve.

In 1961, A.W. Tozer made this sobering lament: "What comes into our minds when we think about God is the most important thing about us."[38] Therefore, how we view God is of paramount importance. The way we view God has important ramifications. Tragically, many people have chosen to either ignore the clear teaching of Scripture or utterly cast aside the biblical portrait of God. J.I. Packer warns, "Disregard the study of God, and you sentence yourself to stumble and blunder through life blindfolded, as it were, with no sense of direction and

[37] G.K. Chesterton, Cited in Ravi Zacharias, A Shattered Visage: The Real Face of Atheism (Brentwood: Wolgemuth & Hyatt Publishers, 1990), 2.

[38] A.W. Tozer, *The Knowledge of the Holy* (Lincoln: Back to the Bible, 1961), 1.

no understanding of what surrounds you. This way you can waste your life and lose your soul."[39] Ignoring Packer's counsel would be exceedingly unwise and foolish. Yet that is exactly what we see on the theological landscape as churches are quick to cave in, which is tantamount to ecclesiastical suicide. "Whoever heeds instruction is on the path to life, but he who rejects reproof leads others astray" (Prov. 10:17). In this chapter, we will discover how the Bible reveals God and contrast this presentation with the dismantled God becoming so popular.

THE TRANSCENDENCE AND IMMANENCE OF GOD

The Bible presents God as both transcendent and immanent. God is *transcendent,* that is, he is over and above his creation. He is distinct and independent of his creation. Our transcendent God sustains all things by his powerful word (Heb. 1:3). He is God and Father of all, who is over all and through all and in all (Eph. 4:6). He is the Creator (Gen. 1:1 Acts 17:24; Isa. 40:28; Col. 1:16). He is sovereign (Exod. 4:11; Ps. 115:3; Prov. 16:33; 21:1). He is the King who reigns over all things and all people (Ps. 98:6; Isa. 44:6). He is the alpha and omega (Isa. 44:6; Rev. 1:8). And our transcendent God is the supreme judge (2 Tim. 4:8).

The transcendence of God is under attack in local churches and has been minimized in a way that dishonors his sovereignty. The chief culprit of this horrible state of affairs is theological liberalism. J. Gresham Machen drove this point home in his landmark work, *Christianity and Liberalism:*

> *The truth is that liberalism has lost sight of the very center and core of the Christian teaching ... one attribute of God is absolutely fundamental in the Bible ... in order to render intelligible all the rest. That attribute is the awful transcendence of God. It is true, indeed, that not a sparrow falls to the ground without Him. But He is immanent in the world not because He is identified with the world, but because He is the free Creator and upholder of it. Between the creature and the Creator a great gulf is fixed.*[40]

---

[39] J.I. Packer, *Knowing God* (Downers Grove: InterVarsity Press, 1973), 17.
[40] J. Gresham Machen, *Christianity and Liberalism* (Edinburgh: Banner of Truth Trust, 1987), 62-63.

Michael Horton observes, "Liberals and revivalists both de-emphasize God's transcendence and tend to see God's Word as something that wells up within a person rather than as something that comes to a person from outside."[41] We are, therefore, left with a false portrait of God—as one who is powerless and has surrendered his authority to the will of the creatures. Such a god is unworthy of worship and unworthy of service. Indeed, such a god is rendered utterly ineffectual. This invention of men is a cheap substitute and is no better than the idols which are routinely condemned in Scripture (Isa. 57:13; Jer. 10:5, 8-9; 16:18; 51:17; Ezek. 20:7-8).

Additionally, God is *immanent,* that is, he gently cares for his people. He is intimately involved with them and delights in meeting their needs. Robert Van de Kapelle and John Curid add, "Yahweh, the Hebrew name for God, an archaic imperfect for the verb 'to be,' also stresses the dynamic, continual presence of God with his people."[42] When considering the immanence of God, we are immediately struck with the most powerful demonstration of this quality: namely, the incarnation of Jesus Christ (John 1:1, 14).

Third, *God is sovereign—people are not.* The Scriptures speak for themselves and beautifully portray a God who is in complete control over all things. Yet, teachers like Bill Johnson give lip service to the sovereignty of God but deny that he controls everything in the universe. Johnson says, "One of our biggest areas of confusion in the church is concerning the sovereignty of God. We know that God is all-powerful. We know that he is in charge of everything. But with that, we make a mistake in thinking he is in control of everything. There's a difference from being in charge and being in control."[43]

But the Word of God is clear on this matter. God is both sovereign over all things *and* in control of all things:

> *Our God is in the heavens; he does all that he pleases (Ps. 115:3).*

[41] Michael Horton, *Christless Christianity: The Alternative Gospel of the American Church*, Kindle edition, Loc. 717.

[42] Cited W. Andrew Hoffecker, Ed. *Building a Christian Worldview* (Phillipsburg: Presbyterian and Reformed Publishing Company, 1986), 16.

[43] https://www.youtube.com/watch?v=zB1BGhvCij4

Many are the plans in the mind of a man, but it is the purpose of the LORD that prevails (Prov. 19:21).

The king's heart is a stream of water in the hand of the LORD; he turns it wherever he will (Prov. 21:1).

Who can speak and have it happen if the Lord has not decreed it? Is it not from the mouth of the Most High that both calamities and good things come? (Lam. 3:37-38, NIV).

All the inhabitants of the earth are accounted as nothing, and he does according to his will among the host of heaven and among the inhabitants of the earth; and none can stay his hand or say to him, 'What have you done?' (Dan. 4:35).

Is a trumpet blown in a city, and the people are not afraid? Does disaster come to a city, unless the LORD has done it? (Amos 3:6).

Charles Haddon Spurgeon understood the importance of embracing the sovereign control of God over all things:

I believe that every particle of dust that dances in the sunbeam does not move an atom more or less than God wishes— that every particle of spray that dashes against the steamboat has its orbit as well as the sun in the heavens—that the chaff from the hand of the winnower is steered as the stars in their courses. The creeping of an aphid over the rosebud is as much fixed as the march of the devastating pestilence—the fall of sere leaves from a poplar is as fully ordained as the tumbling of an avalanche. He that believes in God must believe this truth. There is no standing-point between this and atheism. There is no halfway between a mighty God that worketh all things by the sovereign counsel of his will and no God at all. A God that cannot do as he pleases—a God whose will is frustrated, is not a God, and cannot be a God. I could not believe in a God as that.[44]

Embracing the absolute sovereignty and supremacy of God, then, is critical if we are to have a proper concept of God. This truth

---

[44] *Spurgeon Sermons*—Volume 2, God's Providence, 201.

inevitably clashes with the so-called libertarian free will of the creature which dominates the theological landscape these days. Martin Luther defends the sovereignty of God and denounces the humanistic concept of libertarian free will in his well-known work, *The Bondage of the Will*. Luther writes, "This, therefore, is also essentially necessary and wholesome for Christians to know: that God foreknows nothing by contingency, but that he foresees, purposes, and does all things according to his immutable, eternal, and infallible will. By this thunderbolt, 'Free-will' is thrown prostrate, and utterly dashed to pieces."[45] Luther does not deny human responsibility here. But he does vehemently oppose the notion of libertarian free will, where people are granted the power of contrary choice, irrespective of God's sovereignty. We need to humbly submit to the truth that God is absolutely sovereign and in control. And we must surrender every claim to autonomy.

A BRIEF HISTORY OF GOD'S DEMISE

Despite the clear teaching of Scripture, some people knowingly suppress what Scripture and creation reveal about the God of the universe. "It is unnecessary, we are told, to have a 'conception' of God; theology, or the knowledge of God, it is said, is the death of religion; we should not seek to know God, but should merely feel His presence."[46] In 1966, Time Magazine questioned the very existence of God in the cover article, "*Is God Dead?*" The article reads in part:

> *Is God dead? The three words represent a summons to reflect on the meaning of existence. No longer is the question the taunting jest of skeptics for whom unbelief is the test of wisdom and for whom Nietzsche is the prophet who gave the right answer a century ago ... How does the issue differ from the age-old assertion that God does not and never did exist? Nietzsche's thesis was that striving, self-centered man had killed God, and that settled that. The current death-of-God group believes that God is indeed absolutely dead, but proposes to carry on*

---

[45] Martin Luther, *The Bondage of the Will* (Grand Rapids: Baker Book House, reprint 1976), 38.

[46] J. Gresham Machen, *Christianity and Liberalism* (Grand Rapids: Eerdman's Publishing Company, 1923), 54.

and write a theology without theos, without God. Less radical Christian thinkers hold that at the very least God in the image of man, God sitting in heaven, is dead, and—in the central task of religion today—they seek to imagine and define a God who can touch men's emotions and engage men's minds. [47]

Over fifty years have passed since the popular periodical declared the untimely demise of God.[48] The events of the 60's and 70's helped fuel the fire of the godless and prime the pens of the philosophers. Tragic events like the war in Vietnam, the Watergate scandal, Roe v. Wade, and the Iran hostage crisis helped escalate the collective consciousness of the godless.

The demise of God, while disheartening, was a mere extension of Friedrich Nietzsche's (1844-1900) nihilistic agenda which he aggressively promoted in the nineteenth century. The German philosopher proposed the death of God and led many readers like lambs to the slaughter. His *Parable of the Madman* proposed that "we killed God … we are his murderers."[49]

Al Martin describes how Satan has worked hard to destroy the biblical portrait of God through the agency of liberalism: "One of his great hammer blows was that of religious liberalism, which distorted the God of the Bible and turned Him from the glorious, fearful God of Israel, the God and Father of our Lord Jesus Christ, into a formless mass of unprincipled sentiment called love. His holiness, justice, and righteous anger were largely forgotten if not flatly denied."[50] Liberals continue to advance a vision of God which is out of step with Scripture. The dismantling of God continues with shameless abandon.

A CULTURE OF UNBELIEF

These are some of the consequences of living in a fallen world. Scripture warns us that unrighteous people will suppress the truth of God's existence

---

[47] John T. Elson, *Time Magazine*, 8 April, 1966.

[48] Alistair McGrath discusses the progression of atheism in his excellent work, *The Twilight of Atheism* (Colorado Springs: Waterbrook Press, 2006).

[49] Walter Kaufmann, Ed. *The Portable Nietzsche* (New York: The Viking Press, 1954), 95.

[50] Albert Martin, *The Forgotten Fear: Where Have All the God-Fearers Gone?* (Grand Rapids: Reformation Heritage, 2015), Kindle edition, Loc. 1676.

(Rom. 1:18). It should come as no surprise when atheists come galloping into our world; people who fail to honor God or pay proper respect to him. The Word of God tells us their thought patterns are futile and their hearts are blackened by sin (Rom. 1:22). Fallen people engage in an idolatrous exchange. Paul the apostle says they "exchanged the glory of the immortal God for images resembling mortal man and birds and animals and creeping things" (Rom. 1:23). Scripture says that such people fail to acknowledge God; that "God gave them up to a debased mind to do what ought not to be done" (Rom. 1:28). The Bible warns us that our generation will be filled with unbelief. So, ungodliness should not surprise us. Worldly people will twist the truth and turn from the truth.

DISMANTLING GOD IN THE CHURCH

What comes as a surprise is the dismantling of God in the church. While Scripture paints a vivid portrait of God's nature, sinful people continue to dismantle the God of the Bible (Rom. 1:18). David Wells, for instance, describes the danger of neglecting the transcendence of God: "We put all our eggs, so to speak, in the basket of God's nearness, his relatedness, and we lose everything related to his otherness and transcendence. This yields a God who is familiar, safe, accommodating, but also very small."[51] Such a view misrepresents God and fails to honor him as Scripture demands.

A.W. Tozer was deeply concerned about the dismantling of God which was one of the motivating factors behind his influential book, *A Knowledge of the Holy.* He writes, "It is my opinion that the Christian conception of God current in these middle years of the twentieth century is so decadent as to be utterly beneath the dignity of the Most High God and actually to constitute for professed believers something amounting to a moral calamity."[52] The pattern that Tozer identified in those days continues in our day, even among people who bear the name of Christ.

Whenever a creature denies or dismantles God, he creates substitutes and ends up erecting false gods in place of the living God. This

---

[51] David F. Wells, *The Courage to Be Protestant* (Grand Rapids: Eerdmans Publishing Company, 2008), 120.

[52] A.W. Tozer, *The Knowledge of the Holy,* 2.

pagan demolition is deeply dishonoring to God, of course, and leads people on a path that not only dishonors God; it is a path that leads people to eternal destruction (1 Thess. 1:9-10).

Several popular worldviews militate against the biblical portrait of God. Each of these worldviews stands diametrically opposed to the truth of God's Word. We will briefly examine a host of worldviews which have wormed their way into the church in varying degrees.

Deism

Deism is a worldview that magnifies God's transcendence and mutilates the truth of God's immanence. Some of the Founding Fathers of the United States of America, most notably, Thomas Jefferson, were deists who believed that God created the cosmos and consequently dismissed himself. In this schema, God simply leaves people to fend for themselves. The end result is a God who does not care for his people. Gone are the images of a God who shepherds his people. Since he is not actively involved with his creation, miracles are excluded. The Virgin birth is relegated to nursery rhymes. The deity of Christ is discarded into the ash heap. In deism, God is the great "watchmaker" in the sky who stands aloof and leaves people to their own devices.

Benjamin Franklin embraced a modified version of deism. The famous Founding Father who grew up with a heritage of Puritan theology eventually repudiated his upbringing and replaced it with a sort of self-styled deism. Franklin's biographer, Walter Isaacson says he "was uncomfortable embracing a simple and unenhanced version of deism, the Enlightenment-era creed that reason and the study of nature (instead of divine revelation) tell us all we can know about our Creator … he adopted a creed that would last the rest of his life: a virtuous, morally fortified, and pragmatic version of deism."[53]

Christian Smith and Melinda Lundquist Denton observe a cultural phenomena they refer to as "*moralistic, therapeutic deism*" (MTD). Their research reveals that many American teenagers are fixated on a God who has nothing to do with the God of the Bible. Smith and Lundquist Denton set forth five components of MTD:

[53] Walter Isaacson, *Benjamin Franklin: An American Life* (New York: Simon & Schuster, 2003), 84-85.

1. A God exists who created and ordered the world and watches over human life on earth.

2. God wants people to be good, nice, and fair to each other, as taught in the Bible and by most world religions.

3. The central goal of life is to be happy and to feel good about oneself.

4. God does not need to be particularly involved in one's life except when God is needed to resolve a problem.

5. Good people go to heaven when they die.[54]

Michael Horton explains what the authors uncovered in their research by noting the three-fold meaning of *moralistic, therapeutic deism.*

1. *Moralistic:* "Basically, good people go to heaven when they die; bad people go to hell. Be nice, try to do your best, God will take care of you." Horton describes the typical sentiment of a person who embraces MTD: "If we are good people who have lost our way but with the proper instructions and motivation can become a better person, we need only a life coach, not a redeemer."[55]

2. *Therapeutic:* "God is used as a personal resource rather than known, worshiped, and trusted; Jesus Christ is a coach with a good game plan for our victory rather than a Savior who has already achieved it for us; salvation is more a matter of having our best life now than being saved from God's judgment by God himself; and the Holy Spirit is an electrical outlet we can plug into for power we need to be all that we can be."[56] Horton continues, "Jesus has been dressed up as a corporate CEO, life coach, culture-warrior, political revolutionary, philosopher, co-pilot, co-sufferer, moral example, and partner in fulfilling our personal and social dreams. But in all these ways, we are reducing the

---

[54] Christian Smith with Melinda Lundquist Denton, *Soul Searching: The Religious and Spiritual Lives of American Teenagers* (New York: Oxford University Press, 2005), 162-163.

[55] Michael Horton, *Christless Christianity: The Alternative Gospel of the American Church*, Kindle edition, Loc. 99.

[56] Ibid, Loc. 151.

central character in the drama of redemption to a prop for our own play."[57]

3. *Deism:* "Basically, the message is that God is nice and we are nice, so we should all be nice."[58] The MTD model essentially declares that God's love gobbles up his justice and holiness. Therefore, "the 'good news' offered here eliminates any need for the actual story recorded in the Gospels. If God's love so easily ignores his justice, holiness, and righteousness, then Christ's death on the cross seems like a cruel waste."[59]

The primary way that MTD makes its way into the church is when the people of God embrace the erroneous notion that *man is basically good.* Herein lies the touchstone of secular psychology and anthropology. The implications of this position are remarkable, indeed. If this premise is true, there is no need for a Savior, no need for a cross, and no need for salvation. Such a view has devastating consequences for the Christian life and the gospel of Jesus Christ.

Pantheism

Another worldview that clashes with the transcendence-immanence model is *pantheism.* Pantheism is the virtual opposite of deism and stresses the immanence of God while ignoring his transcendence, all-together. Pantheism promotes the idea that *all is god and god is all.* This destructive worldview not only destroys the personal nature of God; it destroys human dignity. Moreover, pantheism negates the very attributes which are attributed to the God of the Bible.

The latest *Star Wars* film, as of this writing, has grossed over 2.07 billion dollars in box office sales. After seeing the movie, my fourteen-year-old son was able to identify the unbiblical worldview that emerges in this popular film. He said, "There was no distinction between the Creator and the creature. This is a big problem." A big problem indeed! Peter Jones adds,

The Bible warns us not to worship the creation, but to worship and serve only the Creator. The starting point of Gospel truth

---

[57] Ibid, Loc. 233.
[58] Ibid, Loc. 463.
[59] Ibid, Loc. 680.

is that God the Creator, in the three persons of the divine Trinity—Father, Son and Holy Spirit—is the one and only God, and that all which is not God was created by Him … The Christian faith maintains a separateness between God and His creation.[60]

Jones makes it clear that this worldview not only permeates our cultural milieu. He says, "Pagan spirituality has deep roots in Western culture."[61] He highlights a history of religious movements, all of which find their inspiration in pagan spirituality, including Isis Worship, Gnosticism, Free Masonry, Wicca, Buddhism, Jungian Transpersonal Psychology, Sufism, and Magick.[62]

Materialism

Materialism conflicts with the transcendence-immanence model as well. It simply denies the existence of God. *Materialism* makes this audacious claim: the "material universe is all there is." The atheist scientist, Carl Sagan became a household name with his famous quip which appears on the first page of his best-selling book, *Cosmos*. Dr. Sagan writes, "The Cosmos is all that is or was or ever will be. Our feeblest contemplations of the Cosmos stir us—there is a tingling in the spine, a catch in the voice, a faint sensation, as if a distant memory, of falling from a height. We know we are approaching the greatest of mysteries."[63] Such is the hopeless world of the materialist.

Chance rules in the materialistic worldview. There is no purpose in such a universe. It just is. Anyone who questions the notion of a self-caused universe is labeled as uneducated at best and moronic at worst.

Dualism

Dualism is the notion that posits two equal and competing forces in nature—good and evil. This view argues that God does not stand behind evil in any way, shape or form. This would mean that a given event is outside the sovereign control of God. D.A. Carson observes,

[60] Peter Jones, *Gospel Truth, Pagan Lies: Can You Tell the Difference?* (Enumclaw: Winepress Publishing, 1999), 23-24.

[61] Peter Jones, *One or Two: Seeing a World of Difference* (Escondido: Main Entry Editions, 2010), 33.

[62] Ibid, 33-34.

[63] Carl Sagan, *Cosmos* (New York: Ballantine Books Trade, 1980), 1.

"That would mean there is another power, apart from God and outside the domain of God's sovereignty, that challenges him."[64] Dualists reject the biblical teaching that creation was good but became polluted as a result of the Fall. Dualism holds that these two forces of good and evil are equal in power, thus falling dreadfully short of the biblical description of God triumphing over evil.

Pelagianism

Pelagianism is the ancient heresy that originates with Pelagius, a fourth-century British monk who taught that man could attain his own salvation through his own efforts apart from grace. Four tenets of Pelagianism capture the essence of this deviant worldview:

1. He denied that human sin was inherited from Adam.

2. He denied that death is the consequence of Adam's sin.

3. He argued that God predestines no one, except in the sense that he foresees who will believe who will reject his gracious influences.

4. Free will stands at the very center of Pelagian thought.[65]

Alistair McGrath continues,

> *Pelagius taught that the resources of salvation are located within humanity. Individual human beings have the capacity to save themselves. They are not trapped by sin, but have the ability to do all that is necessary to be saved. Salvation is something which is earned through good works, which places God under an obligation to humanity. Pelagius marginalizes the idea of grace, understanding it in terms of demands made of humanity by God in order that salvation may be achieved—such as the Ten Commandments or the moral example of Christ. The ethos of Pelagianism could be summed up as 'salvation by merit,' whereas Augustine taught salvation by grace.*[66]

---

[64] D.A. Carson, *A Call to Spiritual Reformation* (Grand Rapids: Baker Books, 1992), 158.

[65] For a more detailed discussion on Pelagianism, see R.C. Sproul, *Willing to Believe* (Grand Rapids: Baker, 2018).

[66] Alistair McGrath, *Reformation Thought: An Introduction* (Oxford: Blackwell, 1988), 74.

For Pelagius, the command to obey implies the ability to obey. Free will, properly exercised, produces virtue, which is the supreme good and is justly followed by reward. By his own effort, man can achieve whatever is required of him in morality and religion. So, for Pelagius, it would be utterly inconsistent for God to give a command that one could not obey. Making such a command without giving creatures sufficient ability to obey would be the epitome of unfairness in the eyes of Pelagius.

It has been nearly 1,700 years since the birth of Pelagius. Pelagianism was vigorously condemned throughout church history. The third ecumenical council in Ephesus (A.D. 431) held one year after Augustine's death, condemned Pelagianism. While the church rejected Pelagianism as heretical, she slowly drifted back to Pelagianism during the Middle ages—thanks largely to the influence of the Roman Catholic church.

Some theologians were deeply concerned with the doctrinal errors of Pelagianism. Their aim was to forge a middle ground between Pelagianism and Augustinianism. The theological "halfway house" known as Semi-Pelagianism was condemned by the Council of Orange in 529 A.D.[67] However, Semi-Pelagian thought regained momentum and was adopted as the official teaching position of the Roman Catholic Church which stands to this day.

The troubling reality is that many evangelicals embrace the teaching of Semi-Pelagianism. Michael Horton identifies how we naturally gravitate toward theological error: "Hitching our wagon to the spirit of the age, whatever we call it, always leads to one form or another of culture-Christianity—in other words, to our native Pelagianism."[68] Regrettably, we find the lingering tentacles of Pelagianism suffocating the church. Some modern-day Evangelicals have embraced the Pelagian lie that we have an innate ability to accomplish anything (even attain salvation) through our own efforts. Luther identified this diabolical problem in the 16th-century church. "The church," Luther believed, taught that the individuals could gain favor and

---

[67] See Henry Bettenson, *Documents of the Christian Church* (New York: Oxford University Press, 1947), 86-87.

[68] Michael Horton, *Christless Christianity: The Alternative Gospel of the American Church,* Kindle edition, Loc. 1469.

acceptance in the sight of God on account of their personal achievements and status, thus negating the whole idea of grace."[69] Thus, grace is ultimately nullified in the eyes of a well-meaning individual.

Each time sin is minimized, we are reminded of the Pelagian heresy. Each time the free will of the creature is exalted, we recall the Pelagian lie. Whenever the sinner is granted the innate right and ability to believe the gospel apart from grace, we are reminded that Pelagianism is alive and well. Pelagianism has and always will deceive people and makes promises that can never be delivered. Pelagianism makes much of the creature and fails to honor the Creator. As such, this devious theological construct will continue to hinder the progress of the church.

Atheism

The so-called four horsemen of atheism came galloping onto the world stage in the late twentieth century. Mounted sky-high on their horses of atheistic certainty included Richard Dawkins, Christopher Hitchens, Sam Harris, and Daniel Dennett. Each thinker brought his own brand of vitriol to the discussion. And each one agreed that God had been effectively dismantled. The notion of a divine being, in their atheistic framework, is simply not relevant in our age.

Built into the worldview of these men is a deep antipathy to the God of the Bible. For instance, Dawkins maintains that God is a "pernicious delusion" founded on "local traditions of private revelation rather than evidence."[70] The popular Oxford professor caricatures God in horrific terms:

> *The God of the Old Testament is arguably the most unpleasant character in all fiction: jealous and proud of it; a petty, unjust, unforgiving control- freak; a vindictive, bloodthirsty ethnic cleanser; a misogynistic, homophobic, racist, infanticidal, genocidal, filicidal, pestilential, megalomaniacal, sadomasochistic, capriciously malevolent bully.*[71]

The late Christopher Hitchens argued that "religion kills" in his

---

[69] Alistair McGrath, *Reformation Thought: An Introduction* (Oxford: Blackwell, 1993), 33.

[70] Richard Dawkins, *The God Delusion* (Boston: Houghton Mifflin Company, 2006), 31-32.

[71] Ibid, 31.

book, *God is Not Great: How Religion Poisons Everything.*[72] Hitchens continues, "We atheists do not require any priests, or any hierarchy above them, to police our doctrine. Sacrifices and ceremonies are abhorrent to us, as are relics and the worship of any images or objects (even including objects in the form of one of man's most useful innovations: the bound book)."[73] The best-selling British writer believed that one could live a good life without God and ultimately sacrificed the embodiment of truth on the altar of human reason. Such is the fate of a person who denies the existence of God yet seeks to live a virtuous life.

Sam Harris essentially argues that a belief in God defies the laws of reason and rationality. It is this presupposition that led him to write, *The End of Faith: Religion, Terror, and the Future of Reason.* Harris says in the epilogue, "My goal in writing this book has been to help close the door to a certain style of irrationality."[74] Harris admits we live in a "universe shot through with mystery."[75] Yet he adds, "No personal God need be worshiped for us to live in awe at the beauty and immensity of creation."[76] This is the worldview of a thinker who repudiates the existence of God.

Panentheism

Panentheism is a worldview that maintains that all is within God —and it appears to be gaining momentum. In Doug Pagitt's book, *Flipped,* the author sets out to fundamentally transform the classic view of God. The basic idea that runs through this book is what the author refers to as a "flip"—which is nothing short of revising one's views about God, Scripture, and the Christian life in general. Pagitt adds, "The Flip at the center of this book is one that turned me around as a pastor and a Christian writer as well as my personal life and faith."[77]

---

[72] Christopher Hitchens, *God is Not Great: How Religion Poisions Everything* (New York: Hachette Book Group, 2007), 13.

[73] Ibid, 6.

[74] Sam Harris, *The End of Faith: Religion, Terror, and the Future of Reason* (New York: Norton Books, 2004), 223.

[75] Ibid, 227.

[76] Ibid.

[77] Doug Pagitt, *Flipped: The Provocative Truth That Changes Everything We Know About God* (New York: Convergent Books, 2015), 7.

Several "flips" are addressed in this work. But the one that keeps surfacing concerns a fundamental misunderstanding of the nature of God. At the heart of this book is a commitment to panentheism. This worldview, also known as process theology is a radical departure from the traditional understanding of God, yet is receiving a hearing in progressive and liberal churches. One might consider such a view a halfway house between theism and pantheism. But make no mistake—panentheism is outside the scope of historical orthodoxy.

To be fair, the author never uses the word, panentheism. Yet this panentheistic theme runs throughout the book. Pagitt argues, "God is not a separate single subject … If God were not a separate being from all things in the cosmos, then we need not simply say God exists. We can say that God is *existence*. All is in God."[78] Such language is the classic lingo of panentheism.

My initial impression: *Surely this is a typo!* The author can't possibly mean what he is saying. But as I continued to read, my suspicions were confirmed. "… All that exists is In God," writes Pagitt.[79] He tries to justify this "flip" by appealing to the rationale from Acts 17:28 where Paul quotes Epimenides of Crete: "In him we live and move and have our being." This panentheistic scheme is being actively promoted in some churches—yet another indication that the *white flag* flies proudly in the postmodern milieu.

Open Theism

Open theism clings tenaciously to the notion of a God who does not know the future. In spite of the clear teaching of Scripture and the testimony of church history, open theism categorically denies a God who has comprehensive foreknowledge of future events.[80] Indeed, the future is entirely unknown to God, according to advocates of

[78] Ibid, 10-11.
[79] Ibid, 13.
[80] For a thorough treatment of Open Theism, see Bruce A. Ware, *God's Lesser Glory* (Wheaton: Crossway Books, 2000), *Their God is Too Small* (Wheaton: Crossway Books, 2003), John Piper, Justin Taylor, Paul Kjoss Helseth, Ed. *Beyond the Bounds: Open Theism and the Undermining of Biblical Christianity* (Wheaton: Crossway Books, 2003), and John M. Frame, *No Other God: A Response to Open Theism* (Phillipsburg: Presbyterian & Reformed, 2001).

open theism. It would follow, then, that the unknown future cannot be foreordained by God.

The second key plank of open theism is a belief in the libertarian free will of the creature. Clearly, this is an extension of the belief that God lacks comprehensive foreknowledge. Philosopher, William Hasker defines libertarian free will in vivid terms: "An agent is free with respect to a given action at a given time if at that time it is within the agent's power to perform the action and also in the agent's power to refrain from the action."[81] In this view, the individual has ultimate self-determination.

The promotion of open theism in the church as well as Bible Colleges and Seminaries has grown at an alarming pace. Bruce A. Ware cautions followers of Christ to stand alert. He challenges Christians to be on guard against the pernicious effects of this heresy: "To the extent that the openness model of God penetrates our churches, we can anticipate a greatly lessened confidence in God and a much greater temptation to trust in our own insights and abilities."[82] Ware's words, which were published nearly twenty years ago have become a reality as a weakened church has become polluted by the tenets of openness theology. The muddy waters of open theism are yet another indication of the *white flag,* which flies high above the church.

IMPLICATIONS

There are at least five implications which concern the transcendence and immanence of God. First, *the transcendence and immanence of God are taught side-by-side as co-equal truths regarding God's character.* Isaiah 57:15 says, "For thus says the One who is high and lifted up, who inhabits eternity, whose name is Holy: 'I dwell in the high and holy place, and also with him who is of a contrite and lowly spirit, to revive the spirit of the lowly, and to revive the heart of the contrite.'"

Isaiah 40:10-11 also points to the transcendence and immanence of God as co-equal realities: "Behold, the Lord GOD comes

---

[81] William Hasker, "A Philosophical Perspective," in OG, 136-137. Cited in John M. Frame, *No Other God: A Response to Open Theism* (Phillipsburg: Presbyterian & Reformed, 2001), 23.

[82] Bruce A. Ware, *God's Lesser Glory: The Diminished God of Open Theism* (Wheaton: Crossway Books, 2000), 25.

with might, and his arm rules for him; behold, his reward is with him, and his recompense before him. He will tend his flock like a shepherd; he will gather the lambs in his arms; he will carry them in his bosom, and gently lead those that are with young."

And notice, the twin truths of transcendence and immanence emerge in Isaiah 41:8-10: "But you, Israel, my servant, Jacob, whom I have chosen, the offspring of Abraham, my friend; you whom I took from the ends of the earth, and called from its farthest corners, saying to you, 'You are my servant, I have chosen you and not cast you off'; fear not, for I am with you; be not dismayed, for I am your God; I will strengthen you, I will keep you, I will uphold you with my righteous right hand."

Second, *there is a sharp Creator-creature distinction in Scripture.* God the Creator is never to be confused with his creation. He is in no way a part of creation. He stands apart from creation and is completely independent of it. Scripture is clear on this matter: "For by him all things were created, in heaven and on earth, visible and invisible, whether thrones or dominions or rulers or authorities - all things were created through him and for him" (Col. 1:16). It is important to understand that God not only created the cosmos; he did it for his glory. Jonathan Edwards captured this all-important biblical theme in his monumental work, *A Dissertation Concerning the End for Which God Created the World.* He writes, "Hence it will follow, that the moral rectitude of the disposition, inclination, or affection of God CHIEFLY consists in a regard to HIMSELF, infinitely above his regard to all other beings; or, in other words, his holiness consists in this."[83] The Puritan divine continues, "What God says in his word, naturally leads us to suppose, that the way in which he makes himself his end in his work or works, which he does *for his own sake,* is in making *his glory his end.*"[84]

The creation and the creature, on the other hand, are absolutely dependent upon God. Colossians 1:17 says, "And he (Jesus) is before all things, and in him all things hold together." The Greek term,

---

[83] *The Works of Jonathan Edwards*: ed. Edward Hickman, vol. 1, *A Dissertation Concerning the End for Which God Created the World* (Edinburgh: The Banner of Truth Trust, 1834), 98.

[84] Ibid, 107.

sunésteiken or "hold together," means to bring together, and appears in the perfect tense, suggesting an action which took place in the past with results that extend to the present. Paul the apostle continues to explain the absolute dependence of the creature on the Creator in his address to the skeptics in Athens: "The God who made the world and everything in it, being Lord of heaven and earth, does not live in temples made by man, nor is he served by human hands, as though he needed anything, since he gives to all mankind life and breath and everything" (Acts 17:24-25). Paul makes it plain that the Creator is distinct from his creation.

Fourth, *the God of transcendence is not only over and above the scope of the universe and sustaining and controlling all things to the praise of his glory; he is actively involved with his creatures.* He is the Sustainer (Col. 1:17; Heb. 1:3), Healer (2 Chron. 7:14), Law Giver (Exod. 20:1-17), Protector (2 Sam. 22:3), Guide (Ps. 48:14; Isa. 49:10), Comforter (Isa. 40:1), Forgiver (Isa. 43:25; Rom. 5:1), and Shepherd (Ps. 23:1-6; Isa. 40:11). Indeed, he is Immanuel - God with us (Isa. 7:14; John 1:29).

Finally, *the doctrines of transcendence and immanence should cause us to worship, honor, and revere God.* These great realities should prompt rivers of deep humility and reverence to rise within our hearts because we know and experience the God of the universe, who is actively and intimately involved with us. The words of Isaiah 62:5 boldly proclaim God's total involvement with his people: "For as a young man marries a young woman, so shall your sons marry you, and as the bridegroom rejoices over the bride, so shall your God rejoice over you." The sovereign King of the universe finds great delight in meeting the needs of his chosen people.

———————◆———————

We have seen the subtle dismantling of God in culture as well as the compromised church. The history of God's demise is fraught with people who peddle worldly ideas that captivate the attention of people, but ultimately, imprison their souls.

The dismantling of God is a clear indication that the *white flag* flies smugly above the compromised church. The *white flag* is driven by a liberal agenda - either knowingly or unknowingly. Gresham Machen reminds us that liberalism has nothing to do with biblical Christianity: "It is no wonder, then, that liberalism is totally different from Christianity, for the foundation is different. Christianity is founded upon the Bible. It bases upon the Bible both its thinking and its life. Liberalism, on the other hand, is founded upon the shifting emotions of sinful men."[85]

The dismantling of God is only the beginning of our excursion into the walls of the compromised church. We now turn our attention to the crucial matter of the utter disregard for doctrine.

---

[85] J. Gresham Machen, *Christianity and Liberalism*, 79.

4

Disregarding Doctrine

"Those who do away with doctrine ... are the worst enemies of Christian living."

C.H. SPURGEON

THE DOCTRINAL DIVIDE

The date was May 1994. I was waiting patiently for the rehearsal to begin for my Seminary commencement. As I made good use of my time by pouring over an interesting book, one of my classmates approached me and asked, "What are you reading?" When I told him that it was a book about a particular doctrinal issue, his face grew downcast. He uttered a few words that I shall not soon forget: "Now that I'm out of this place, I'll never read another book about doctrine again."

The response of my classmate is not unusual. There is a movement afoot in the church that places a high value on feelings and downplays doctrinal matters. "Doctrine divides," they say. "What matters most is sincerity." Their cry is, "Just give me Jesus. Keep the doctrine to yourself."

The apostle Paul warns Timothy to beware of anyone who is promoting false doctrine:

If anyone teaches a different doctrine and does not agree with the sound words of our Lord Jesus Christ and the teaching (didaskalia) that accords with godliness, he is puffed up with conceit and understands nothing. He has an unhealthy craving for controversy and for quarrels about words, which produce envy, dissension, slander, evil suspicions, and constant friction among people who are depraved in mind and deprived of the truth, imagining that godliness is a means of great gain (1 Tim. 6:3-5).

Whenever we succumb to the world by disregarding doctrine, the enemy gains a foothold and the church is weakened as a result. Paul urges Timothy, *"Persist in this, for by so doing you will save both yourself and your hearers"* (1 Tim. 4:6b). Persist (*epiménō*), a present active imperative verb means to "persevere or stay on course."[86] We persevere by continually scrutinizing our lives and our doctrine. The result is important: We will save ourselves and our hearers.

NO CREED BUT CHRIST

Tragically, the church continues to disregard doctrine in droves. Over and over again, we hear the droning tag line, *"No creed but Christ."* It sounds slick. It sounds trendy. It even sounds biblical and evangelical because of the prominent display of Christ's name. However, it is time to rethink this popular mantra for it is, yet another symptom of the *white flag.*

Initially, the slogan *"No creed but Christ"* may seem innocent enough. It appears to give Christ his proper place in the church. It seems to rightly place him at the center of the Christian life. But is it possible this slogan is at its root the very antithesis of all that is Christian and all that honors Christ?

Consider some of the serious implications of this popular slogan: First, imagine where the church would be if Athanasius would have chosen to adopt the slogan, *"No creed but Christ."* In this case,

---

[86] Swanson, J. (1997). Dictionary of Biblical Languages with Semantic Domains: Greek (New Testament) (electronic ed.). Oak Harbor: Logos Research Systems, Inc.

the 4th-century bishop would have refused to quibble over one iota. And as a result, Arianism would have assaulted the church with its godless Christology and emerged the victor.

Second, the slogan leaves us wondering which "Christ" is referred to. Is this "creedless Christ" the figure portrayed in Islam, who is regarded as a mere prophet but stripped of his deity and majesty? Or is he the Christ of Arianism, a mere created being whose blood is insufficient to forgive sinners? Is he the Jesus of modern-day liberalism—the "hipster Jesus" who tolerates sin and changes his mind about hell and eternal punishment?

Disregarding doctrine is another way *the white flag of compromise* is being hoisted high in the church. This aversion to doctrine or theology appears in several forms:

1. Some postmodernists maintain that there is no such thing as absolute truth. Therefore, doctrinal propositions are nonsensical.

2. Relativists argue that truth is culturally conditioned and changing. Therefore, to maintain that one can find truth is presumptuous at best and arrogant at worst.

3. False teachers challenge doctrinal assertions with their own variety of false doctrine. Scripture warns, *"If anyone teaches a different doctrine and does not agree with the sound words of our Lord Jesus Christ and the teaching that accords with godliness, he is puffed up with conceit and understands nothing …"* (1 Tim. 6:3-4a).

4. Some create barriers for the mind that prevent the promotion of a solid doctrinal framework. God's Word says, *"I appeal to you, brothers, to watch out for those who cause divisions and create obstacles contrary to the doctrine that you have been taught; avoid them"* (Rom. 16:17).

5. Some people rail against the notion of sound doctrine or orthodoxy and make an appeal to ecumenicalism—a movement we must resist with all our might.

6. The capitulators of this generation will do everything possible to pry our minds away from doctrinal truth by embracing the spirit of the age—the *zeitgeist*.

1 Timothy 4:1-16 drives home the importance of doctrine. The Greek word, *didaskalia* is translated as "teaching" or "doctrine" and may be used as a means of providing instruction.[87] Scripture makes it clear that God has equipped some believers with the special gift of teaching, which suggests a commitment to the dissemination of doctrine or theology (1 Cor. 12:28).

Ephesians 4:11-12 notes how God presents apostles, prophets, evangelists, shepherds and teachers to "equip the saints for the work of the ministry, for building up the body of Christ." This kind of ministry involves sound doctrinal instruction. The result of this commitment to doctrinal instruction is set forth in verses 13 and 14, namely - that the people of God *"all attain to the unity of the faith and of the knowledge of the Son of God, to mature manhood, to the measure of the stature of the fullness of Christ, so that we may no longer be children, tossed to and fro by the waves and carried about by every wind of doctrine (didaskalia), by human cunning, by craftiness in deceitful schemes."* Observe that this faithful doctrinal instruction aims to prevent being confused and lured away by false doctrine. The principle that emerges here is that everyone has a commitment to some kind of doctrine—either sound doctrine or doctrine that damns.

It is a great mystery why so many people in the church have a predisposition to flee from doctrine or cast stones at anyone who faithfully trains others in the ways of sound doctrine. However, the church that ignores or minimizes doctrine does so at its own peril.

Additionally, Paul instructs believers to provide instruction which is an exercise in doctrinal faithfulness (Rom. 12:7). In 1 Timothy 1:3-4, Paul warns Timothy about the dangers of false doctrine: *"As I urged you when I was going to Macedonia, remain at Ephesus so that you may charge certain persons not to teach any different doctrine, nor to devote themselves to myths and endless genealogies, which promote speculations rather than the stewardship from God that is by faith."*

---

[87] Swanson, J. (1997). Dictionary of Biblical Languages with Semantic Domains: Greek (New Testament) (electronic ed.). Oak Harbor: Logos Research Systems, Inc.

Paul warns Timothy that some will depart from the faith by devoting themselves to deceitful spirits and teachings (*didaskalia*) of demons (v. 1). The apostle admonishes Timothy to be a good steward of Christ. In order to do so, he must be trained in the words of the faith and of the good doctrine (1 Tim. 4:6-7). In other words, the challenge for Timothy is to be trained or nourished by sound doctrine. The challenge is no less crucial for each of us.

Timothy is challenged to "toil" and "strive" (v. 10). The aim of this vigorous effort is doctrinal in nature. Indeed, the aim of this battle for right doctrine is because "we have our hope set on the living God." Right doctrine is to be coupled with right living. Of course, embracing sound doctrine is no guarantee of a godly life. However, godliness will never become a reality apart from sound doctrine. The kinds of propositions we believe and cherish have a direct bearing on the way we live our lives.

In verses 11-13, Paul introduces three imperatives. Timothy is to devote himself to:

1.   The public reading of Scripture—followed by biblical exposition.

2.   Exhortation—challenging believers to apply God's Word to their lives.

3.   Teaching (*didaskalia*)—systematic presentation of doctrine.

WATCH YOUR LIFE AND DOCTRINE

Paul concludes the fourth chapter of 1 Timothy with a bold challenge to the young pastor: "Keep a close watch on yourself and on the teaching. Persist in this, for by so doing you will save both yourself and your hearers" (1 Tim. 4:16). Notice two critical imperatives that emerge in this passage.

Scrutinizing Our Lives

First, Paul instructs Timothy, "Watch your life and doctrine closely" (NIV). Timothy is called upon to scrutinize his life. The imperative means to "pay close attention." The term is written in the present tense which points to ongoing activity. We must scrutinize our lives constantly.

Scrutinizing is not an all-together negative task. Several years ago, I took my car for a routine oil change. Later in the day, I saw oil seeping through my hood and onto the windshield. I quickly discovered after further investigation that the mechanic forgot to replace the cover when he finished dispensing the oil! It should come as no surprise, then, to learn that my new habit is to check the lid after each and every oil change. I am committed to scrutinizing the work of my mechanic.

Scrutinizing our lives is important because we were saved for a specific purpose. Scripture describes this purpose in several places:

> ... even as he chose us in him before the foundation of the world, that we should be holy and blameless before him (Eph. 1:4).

> ... but as he who called you is holy, you also be holy in all your conduct, since it is written, "You shall be holy, for I am holy" (1 Pet. 1:15–16).

> But you are a chosen race, a royal priesthood, a holy nation, a people for his own possession, that you may proclaim the excellencies of him who called you out of darkness into his marvelous light (1 Pet. 2:9).

Paul instructs Timothy, "Train yourself for the purpose of godliness ... godliness is of value in every way, as it holds promise for the present life and also for the life to come" (1 Tim. 4:7b-8).

As noted above, right living is always connected with right doctrine. The apostle Paul says to the believers in Colossae:

> And so, from the day we heard, we have not ceased to pray for you, asking that you may be filled with the knowledge of his will in all spiritual wisdom and understanding, so as to walk in a manner worthy of the Lord, fully pleasing to him, bearing fruit in every good work and increasing in the knowledge of God (Col. 1:9-11; cf. 1 Thess. 4:1-7; 2 Tim. 3:10).

In other words, we need to *know* in order to *grow*. We must acknowledge and embrace doctrine in order to live a fruitful Christian life. John Calvin adds, "And teaching will be of little worth if there is not a corresponding uprightness and holiness of life."[88] Such a fruitful life is necessarily linked to sound doctrine.

Scrutinizing Our Doctrine

Second, Paul instructs Timothy and all subsequent believers to "keep a close watch on the teaching" (*didaskalia*). We are therefore called to scrutinize our doctrine. We are to pay close attention to our doctrine, much like a sentinel stands guard over a precious treasure (Ps. 19:7-11). We make a commitment to guard our orthodoxy. We resolve to never compromise the truth!

Sound doctrine is important for several reasons:

1. It is profitable. "All Scripture is breathed out by God and profitable for teaching, for reproof, for correction, and for training in righteousness, that the man of God may be complete, equipped for every good work" (2 Tim. 3:16; cf. Ps. 19:11).

2. We are commanded to teach what accords with sound doctrine (1 Tim. 4:13; Titus. 2:1).

3. It is the means of encouragement and hope. "For whatever was written in the former days was written for our instruction (*didaskalian*), that through endurance and through the encouragement of the Scriptures we might have hope" (Rom. 15:4).

4. It enables us to be good servants of Christ. "If you put these things before the brothers, you will be a good servant of Christ Jesus, being trained in the words of the faith and of the good doctrine that you have followed" (1 Tim. 4:6).

5. It guards us against false doctrine (Eph. 4:14; 2 Tim. 4:3).

6. It guards us from apostasy (1 Tim. 4:1).

7. It helps us recognize false doctrine (1 Tim. 6:3).

8. It helps us refute those who oppose sound doctrine (Tit. 1:9).

---

[88] John Calvin, *Calvin's New Testament Commentaries—2 Corinthians, Timothy, Titus, Philemon* (Grand Rapids: Eerdmans, 1964), 248.

Please remember this fundamental reality: There is no salvation apart from doctrine. The apostle Paul writes, "Keep a close watch on yourself and on the teaching. Persist in this, for by so doing you will save both yourself and your hearers" (1 Tim. 4:16). Christianity is not a contentless faith. Rather, it is one that sets forth truth in propositions. Donald Bloesch observes, "There can be no vital spirituality, without a sound theology."[89]

BARRIERS THAT PREVENT US FROM SCRUTINIZING OUR DOCTRINE

Any number of things will prevent us from scrutinizing our doctrine. Tolerance is a massive barrier in our postmodern age that prevents us from scrutinizing our doctrine. We tend to erroneously reason with the secularist that rejection of error is tantamount to judgmentalism at best - and arrogance at worst.

Laziness is a powerful force that hinders evangelical sensibilities. In 1 Timothy 4:6, Paul encourages the young pastor for his faithfulness in following the good doctrine. In other words, Timothy gave careful attention to doctrine. He scrutinized his doctrine. Laziness actually prevents us from following in Timothy's footsteps. Tragically, some believers pay closer attention to the box scores, stock market, or the latest plot in a mini-series on television than to sound doctrine.

Some of us are simply unconvinced about the importance of doctrine. One theologian warns us, "A healthy Christianity cannot survive without theology, and theology must matter today, especially in our mindless and irrational culture."[90] Yet a growing number of Christians apparently see little if any need to focus our attention on the great doctrinal realities of Scripture.

We may be sidelined by humanism. Anyone who falls prey to the tenets of humanism should remember Paul's warning in 2 Timothy 4:3-4. The apostle writes, "For the time is coming when people will not endure sound teaching, but having itching ears they will ac-

---

[89] Donald Blotch, *Crumbling Foundations: Death & Rebirth in an Age of Upheaval* (Grand Rapids: Academic Books, 1984), 111. Cited in John H. Armstrong, *The Coming Evangelical Crisis* (Chicago: Moody Press, 1996), 57.

[90] Gary Johnson, Cited in John H. Armstrong, *The Coming Evangelical Crisis* (Chicago: Moody Press, 1996), 57.

cumulate for themselves teachers to suit their own passions, and will turn away from listening to the truth and wander off into myths."

The spiritual tsunami culture we live in is on the lookout for doctrinal compromisers and capitulators. But we maintain our commitment to the truth by scrutinizing our lives and doctrine. We must resolve to stand firm in this mandate.

B.B. Warfield understood the importance of maintaining biblical standards in a compromised world:

> *Convictions are the root on which the tree of vital Christianity grows. No convictions, no Christianity. Scanty convictions, hunger-bitten Christianity. Profound convictions, solid and substantial religion. Let no one fancy that it can be otherwise. Ignorance is not the mother of religions but of irreligion. The knowledge of God is eternal life, and to know God means that we know Him aright.*[91]

Oh, that we would nurture biblical convictions which are rooted in sound doctrine. May our rock-solid convictions magnify God, exalt the Lord Jesus Christ, and rejoice in the sovereignty of God. Oh, that we would proclaim a set of doctrinal standards that accurately articulate the gospel and resounds in praise to the Lord Jesus Christ! Spurgeon says, "Truth could not be truth in this world if it were not a warring thing, and we should at once suspect that it were not true if error were friends with it. The spotless purity of truth must always be at war with the blackness of heresy and lies."[92] May we strive to be a people of the truth by refusing to disregard doctrine any longer.

If the thought of comparing this "creedless Christ" to a hodgepodge of world religions sparks any concerns, consider the essence of the phrase. It could actually mean just about anything.

---

[91] B.B. Warfield, Selected Shorter Writings, 1:376. Cited in John H. Armstrong, *The Coming Evangelical Crisis* (Chicago: Moody Press, 1996), 67.

[92] C.H. Spurgeon, Cited in John MacArthur, *The Truth War: Fighting for Certainty in an Age of Deception*, v.

The term "creed" comes from the Latin, which means, "I believe." Therefore, this "creedless Christ" could mean anything one wants to believe.

If the slogan, "No creed but Christ" is truly valid, then this notion renders the imperative to catechize believers utterly meaningless. Scripture stands opposed to such a view:

> *But you, beloved, building yourselves up in your most holy faith and praying in the Holy Spirit ... (Jude 20).*

> *Therefore, as you received Christ Jesus the Lord, so walk in him, rooted and built up in him and established in the faith, just as you were taught, abounding in thanksgiving (Col. 2:6–7).*

> *But as for you, teach what accords with sound doctrine (Titus 2:1).*

> *He had been instructed in the way of the Lord. And being fervent in spirit, he spoke and taught accurately the things concerning Jesus, though he knew only the baptism of John (Acts 18:25).*

Additionally, the great gladiators of the Christian faith agree that catechizing is an essential element of discipleship. John Bunyan writes, "But the composition of a catechism was found to require the clearest conception of truth, and the fullest command of simple, expressive phraseology." Spurgeon adds, "I am persuaded that the use of a good Catechism in all our families will be a great safeguard against the increasing errors of the times."

Next, the slogan, "No creed but Christ" is self-refuting. The very statement is a proposition. Yet this kind of creed bemoans propositions, reacts to doctrinal statements, and discounts theological systems. In the end, the dogmatic slogan, "No creed but Christ" becomes a sort of theological system!

At best, the slogan, "No creed but Christ" is naive. Tragically, a host of well-intentioned Christians have failed to think through the implications of such a statement. And the fertile soil of naivety, though well-intentioned, may cultivate theological error and produce thorns and thistles in the Christian life.

At worst, the slogan is arrogant and drips with theological hubris. To discount the foundational creeds of historic Christianity is always a step in the wrong direction. Indeed, to cast aside the historic creeds is to do violence to the nature of faith itself. Consider the following creedal statements that describe fundamental Christological realities:

> … *Jesus Christ, the only-begotten Son of God, begotten of the Father before all worlds, God of God, light of Light, very God of very God, begotten, not made, being of one substance with the Father; by whom all things were made (The Nicene Creed, 325 A.D.)*

> … *Our Lord Jesus Christ, the same perfect Godhead and also perfect in manhood; truly God and truly man, of a reasonable soul and body … (Chalcedonian Creed, 451 A.D.)*

> *The Father uncreated: the Son uncreated: and the Holy Spirit uncreated (The Athanasian Creed, 4th-5th centuries, A.D.)*

The not so subtle trend in the church is to move away from doctrine. We see this at every juncture, especially in churches where postmodernity has taken root. Spurgeon stated emphatically, "Those who do away with doctrine … are the worst enemies of Christian living."[93]

A creedless Christ, is in fact, a creedless Christianity which is something akin to a toothless tiger whose motives may be noble, but will ultimately be ravaged by his enemies. Paul warned, "I know that after my departure fierce wolves will come in among you, not sparing the flock; and from among your own selves will arise men speaking twisted things, to draw away the disciples after them" (Acts 20:29-30). It should be noted that Paul's concern at this juncture was false doctrine and worldly philosophy that would come from within the church walls. The apostle continues, "Therefore be alert, remembering that for three years I did not cease night or day to admonish every one with tears" (Acts 20:31).

Our challenge is to heed Paul's warning and be on the lookout for both doctrinal deceivers and those who disregard doctrine. The next

---

[93] Cited in Erroll Hulse and David Kingdon, eds., *A Marvelous Ministry: How the All-Round Ministry of Charles Haddon Spurgeon Speaks to Us Today* (Ligonier, PA: Soli Deo Gloria, 1993), 128. John Piper, *A Camaraderie of Confidence* (Wheaton: Crossway Books, 2016), 38.

time you hear a well-intentioned person promote a "No creed but Christ" worldview, remember that godly people devoted their lives to hammer out the creeds and confessions in order to build up the church and protect the flock from theological wolves. The creeds were carefully and prayerfully fashioned so we might know and worship Christ rightly. This Christ is the uncreated One who himself created all things (Col. 1:16). He was born of the Virgin Mary (Luke 1:26-35), tempted in all ways as we are, yet without sin (Heb. 4:15; 1 Pet. 2:21-24). This Savior perfectly obeyed the law of God, died on the cross for sinners, and was raised on the third day for our justification (1 Cor. 15:3-5; Rom. 4:25; Acts 2:22-24). This Savior is fully God and fully man and stood in the place of everyone who would ever believe (Gal. 3:13; Isa. 53:4-6). This Substitute bore our sins (2 Cor. 5:21), satisfied the wrath of God (Rom. 3:23-26), redeemed us from the slave market of sin, rescued us from hell (Col. 1:13-14), and reconciled us to God (Rom. 5:10). This Savior is worthy of our undivided allegiance, devotion, and worship!

5

Denigrating the Work of Christ

———◇———

"Yet because of false brothers secretly brought in—who slipped in to spy out our freedom that we have in Christ Jesus, so that they might bring us into slavery— to them we did not yield in submission even for a moment, so that the truth of the gospel might be preserved for you."

GALATIANS 2:4-5

So far, we have witnessed a compromised church that is dismantling God and disregarding doctrine. The *white flag* is rising steadily as the church witnesses her effectiveness decline and her faithfulness falter.

Another feature of the compromised church is *denigrating the work of Christ*. This act of denigration involves trivializing or undervaluing Christ's work on the cross. When we denigrate someone, we mock them; we scorn them; we ridicule them. Anyone who denigrates the cross-work of Christ places themselves in a position of self-imposed power. The act of denigration, then, is an act of idolatry, which kindles the holy wrath of Almighty God (Col. 3:5-6).

Denigrating the work of Christ comes in many forms. For instance, anyone who repudiates the penal substitutionary atonement of Christ denigrates his sacrificial work. J. Gresham Machen writes, "… We know absolutely nothing about an atonement that is not a vicarious atonement, for that is the only atonement of which the New Testament speaks."[94] Yet professing Christians are increasingly denying the substitutionary atonement. One individual who embraces the moniker, "evangelical liberal" discusses his view of the atonement: "I believe in the atonement for sin made by Jesus on the cross. However, I consider penal substitution to be only one partial and imperfect model for how that atonement 'works.' I also believe God's salvation to be far broader and deeper than a plan to get (some) individual souls into heaven, or to improve our personal morality."[95]

In his book, *A Better Atonement: Beyond the Depraved Doctrine of Original Sin*, Tony Jones writes, "I'm on no quest to reject the penal substitutionary theory of the atonement (PSA). (I merely intend to dethrone it)."[96] However, what he fails to see is this: when penal substitutionary atonement is dethroned, the gospel of Jesus Christ is relegated to the rubbish bin and the hope of every believing person perishes.

Jones makes it abundantly clear in his book, *Did God Kill Jesus?* that he along with other liberals have "grown increasingly uncomfortable with the regnant interpretation of Jesus' death as primarily the propitiation of a wrathful God."[97] Yet, when we reduce the cross to a mere display of love and refuse to acknowledge that Jesus bore the wrath of God, the gospel is utterly stripped of its saving power. Such a move denigrates the very heart of the atonement, which at best compromises the gospel and at worst, destroys it altogether.

Anyone who stands with the Sadducees and denies the resurrection is guilty of denigrating the work of Christ. While we may be far removed from the days of the Sadducees, some of the primary beliefs are still celebrated by people in the church.

The apostle Paul directly confronted people who denied the reality of Christ's resurrection:

---

94 J. Gresham Machen, *Christianity and Liberalism*, 117.
95 https://evangelicalliberal.wordpress.com/creed/
96 Tony Jones, *A Better Atonement: Beyond the Depraved Doctrine of Original Sin* (Minneapolis: The JoPa Group, 2012), Kindle edition, Loc. 297.
97 Tony Jones, *Did God Kill Jesus?* (New York: HarperCollins, 2015), 27.

Now if Christ is proclaimed as raised from the dead, how can some of you say that there is no resurrection of the dead? But if there is no resurrection of the dead, then not even Christ has been raised. And if Christ has not been raised, then our preaching is in vain and your faith is in vain (1 Cor. 15:12–14).

The blatant repudiation of the resurrection of Jesus is not only foolish, such a denial will be met with the fiery judgment of God's wrath against sin.

Another example of denigrating the work of Christ is the ancient heresy of Patripassianism. This God-dishonoring heresy acknowledges "that Christ is fully God, but does not identify the Son as a separate Person, distinct from the Father."[98] This view posits that God the Father actually suffered on the cross.

Whenever the view is advanced that the Father suffered with the Son on the cross, we must immediately recall the importance of the distinction among the Persons in the Trinity. A.W. Pink captures the essence of the truth of abandonment: "And it was because the Savior was bearing our sins that the thrice holy God would not look on him, turned his face from him, forsook him. The Lord made to meet on Christ the iniquities of us all: and our sins being on him as our substitute, the divine wrath against our offenses must be spent upon our sin offering."[99] To embrace and promote the theory of Patripassianism, then, brings reproach to the gospel and casts doubt on its truthfulness and integrity.

If God the Father does not abandon the Son, he surely cannot pour out the full measure of his wrath; hence the doctrine of propitiation is compromised and the gospel message collapses. Thus, the work of Christ is in disrepute. The work of Christ in this instance, then, is denigrated.

THE GOSPEL IS ILLUSTRATED

Interestingly, the apostles did not force Titus to be circumcised. There was no disparity between Paul's gospel and the gospel of the other apostles. The response of the Judaizers is a totally different proposi-

---

[98] Harold O.J. Brown, *Heresies: Heresy and Orthodoxy in the History of the Church* (Peabody: Hendrickson Publishers, 1984), 85.

[99] A.W. Pink, *The Seven Sayings of the Savior on the Cross* (Grand Rapids: Baker Books, 1984), 78.

tion, however. Their response to this uncircumcised Christ-follower is a window into the heart of the legalist. These self-righteous pulpit-pounders wanted people to see a contradiction between Paul and the apostles in Jerusalem.

So, Titus stands in as an object lesson or a case study for the truth of the gospel. He teaches us a lesson which occurs later in Paul's letter to the Galatian believers: "For in Christ Jesus neither circumcision nor uncircumcision counts for anything, but only faith working through love" (Gal. 5:6). Luther observes, "And who is such an uneducated grammarian that he cannot understand from the force of the words that being justified is one thing and working is another?"[100] Luther concludes his thoughts on Galatians 5:6 by exposing the first-century heresy:

> And yet nothing is more contemptible than this very faith and love among those who claim to be the most Christian and to be actually a holier church than the holy church of God itself. On the other hand, they admire and boast of their masquerade and sham of self-chosen works, under which they nourish and conceal their horrible idolatry, wickedness, greed, filth, hatred, murder, and the whole kingdom of hell and the devil. So powerful is the might of hypocrisy and superstition in every age, from the beginning to the end of the world.[101]

Luther draws a line in the sand with the apostles, making it clear that we stand forgiven of all our sins on account of Christ's completed work on our behalf. To add to Christ's work invites theological treason. Such is the crime of anyone who denigrates the work of Christ.

THE GOSPEL IS ATTACKED

Notice how the gospel comes under siege here: "Yet because of false brothers secretly brought in—who slipped in to spy out our freedom that we have in Christ Jesus so that they might bring us into slavery …" (Gal. 2:4). Three specific things stand out as we examine this covert operation designed to undermine the gospel.

[100] Martin Luther, *Luther's Works - Volume 27* (St. Louis: Concordia Publishing House, 1964), 28.
[101] Ibid, 31.

Their identity—These people are false brothers. The term *pseudàdelfos* refers to anyone who pretends to be a member of a given group. The apostle Paul includes "false brothers" among the list of dangerous things in 2 Corinthians 11:22-27. In verse 26, he specifically mentions "danger from rivers, danger from robbers, danger from my own people, danger from Gentiles, danger in the city, danger in the wilderness, danger at sea, danger from false brothers" (*pseudàdelfos*). So there was, no doubt, an element of danger here.

Their strategy—They slipped in secretly. Like the false teachers that Jude addressed who "*crept in unnoticed*" (Jude 4), these gospel mutilators utilized the art of stealth. They crept in and nobody even noticed. They flew under the radar and used deceptive means to accomplish their mission. Like a well-trained mole on a merciless mission, these imposters maneuvered their way into the church.

Their mission—The purpose of their secret entry among the people of God is also spelled out in Galatians 2:4. They "slipped in to spy out our freedom that we have in Christ Jesus so that they might bring us into slavery." Specifically, they were mandating that Gentile believers get circumcised. Such an action would render a Christ-follower a slave to his former way of life. Whenever a condition is added to grace, a professing believer becomes a slave to that condition. Whenever we abandon the gospel of grace, we abandon Christ!

Paul's response is instructive and should be the first inclination of every follower of Jesus: "… to them we did not yield in submission even for a moment, so that the truth of the gospel might be preserved for you" (Gal. 2:5). Paul in effect says, "I will not abandon the gospel. I will not abandon grace. I will never abandon my allegiance to the gospel of the Lord Jesus Christ!"

THE GOSPEL IS AFFIRMED

The leaders in Jerusalem affirm Paul's message by granting him the right hand of fellowship. The men who were pillars of the faith community "perceived the grace that was given to me," writes Paul (Gal. 2:9). Notice the result: When the message is affirmed, it continues to advance. That is, some go to the Gentiles (the uncircumcised) and some go to the Jews (the circumcised).

Whenever the gospel advances, good things happen. Hospitals and homes are built. Hungry people are fed. The poor are clothed and addictions are conquered. Sinful habits are broken. People are made right with God, their sins are forgiven, and their lives are transformed!

Another common way of denigrating the work of Christ is to add to grace. Throughout the history of the church, we have seen the false addition of works to the free grace which is ours in Christ. The apostle Paul experienced the first-hand assault on grace in Galatians 2:1-10. We will witness how Paul drew a line in the sand as he encountered the legalistic schemes of the Judaizers.

THE GOSPEL IS ON DISPLAY

The book of Acts indicates that Paul visited Jerusalem at least four times.[102] The first trip occurred shortly after his conversion (Acts 9:26-30). His conversion was so fresh in the mind of the disciples (who still knew Paul as Saul), that they were actually afraid of him. But Barnabas stood strong with his new friend and boldly preached the Word of God in Jerusalem (Acts 9:28). When Paul's life was threatened by the Hellenists (Greek-speaking Jews), his new friends sent him north to Tarsus (Acts 9:30). Acts 9:31 gives us an inside look at the excitement that is building toward the gospel which was on display: "So the church throughout all Judea and Galilee and Samaria had peace and was being built up. And walking in the fear of the Lord and in the comfort of the Holy Spirit, it multiplied."

The purpose of the second trip was to take a gift to the poor who had endured a famine (Acts 11:27-30). The third trip became known as the Jerusalem Council (Acts 15:1ff). At this council, the Gentiles were formally welcomed into the church. The fourth trip ultimately led to the arrest of Paul when he was finally sent to Rome (Acts 21-28).

Commentators disagree as to whether Galatians 2:1-10 refers to Paul's second or third trip to Jerusalem. For our purposes, let us move our focus from the timing of the events to the actual event itself.

In Galatians 2:1, we find three men who arrive on the scene in Jerusalem. Both Paul and Barnabas were Jews; Titus was Greek (remem-

---

[102] See Phillip Graham Ryken, *Galatians: Reformed Expository Commentary* (Phillipsburg: Presbyterian and Reformed, 2005), 41.

ber that Greeks were not circumcised). Paul describes the reason for the journey to Jerusalem: "I went up because of a revelation and set before them (though privately before those who seemed influential) the gospel that I proclaim among the Gentiles, in order to make sure I was not running or had not run in vain." In other words, these men made their way to Jerusalem because God told them to go. Why would God send two Jews and a Greek man into the heart of Jerusalem? I believe God sent these men to Jerusalem to put the gospel on display.

Paul labored to help the Galatians understand that sinners may stand innocent in God's sight. That is to say, they may be justified by grace alone through faith alone. He stands side-by-side with Timothy, an uncircumcised Christ-follower in a Jewish culture.[103]

———————————◆———————————

When Paul comes face-to-face with false teachers who denigrate the gospel, he draws a line in the sand. He understands the implications of denying the truth of Christ's substitutionary atonement. He understands that the truth of the gospel is at stake.

What about you? What lines need to be drawn or redrawn in your life? Where do you need to stand up for the truth of the gospel? How can you proclaim the truth of the gospel? Where can you defend these precious realities?

It is time for Christ-followers to embrace, promote, and proclaim the great reality of the gospel. Now is the time to stand your ground and refuse to yield to the grace-robbers. Now is the time to take the gospel to the people who God has called you to minister to.

May you boldly draw the line in the sand by displaying the gospel, defending the gospel, and declaring the gospel to every tribe and every nation! May the cry of every Christ-follower echo the patriot Patrick Henry who cried out, "Give me liberty or give me death!" May you grow strong in your doctrinal convictions as you spread the

———————————

[103] The rite of circumcision was vitally important to the Jews (Gen. 17:9-14). Ever since Genesis 17, the removal of the male foreskin had been the defining mark of the people of God. This mark indicated whether or not a person was inside or outside the covenant.

gospel of grace to people who need to hear the old, old story. And may you refuse to pledge allegiance to the *white flag* of compromise.

"And they sang a new song, saying, 'Worthy are you to take the scroll and to open its seals, for you were slain, and by your blood you ransomed people for God from every tribe and language and people and nation, and you have made them a kingdom and priests to our God, and they shall reign on the earth'" (Rev. 5:9-10).

6

Discarding the Judgment of Christ

◆

"Whoever believes in the Son has eternal life; whoever does not obey the Son shall not see life, but the wrath of God remains on him."

JOHN 3:36

Another way the *white flag* has been hoisted high in the church is the matter of eternal judgment. Theologians and pastors in church history faithfully taught that Christ would judge unbelievers eternally; that they would pay the ultimate penalty for their sins in hell. Yet, many in the contemporary church either resist this teaching or recoil at the very notion of a God who would judge unbelievers for any length of time. The compromised church is growing more and more comfortable with discarding the judgment of Christ.

Several years ago, I met a pastor at a prayer retreat. Later in the evening, he noticed a book I was reading about the wrath of God. After inquiring about the content of the book, he quickly opined: "I don't think God is a God of wrath." The tone in his voice was adamant; his body language uncomfortable. When I asked how he could believe such a thing, his next statement was equally shocking:

"I do not think God is angry with anyone," he said. He went on to promote the popular notion that Jesus came not to demonstrate the justice of God but our sense of justice as humans.

My interaction with this pastor is not an isolated incident. Christian leaders have and will continue to promote the unbiblical notion of a God who accepts all and judges none. This inaccurate belief is based on what people *want* God to be like, not on how the Scriptures actually portray him. We must constantly guard against the tendency to fabricate God in the image of man and sugarcoat the difficult doctrines such as eternal punishment. Just because a given doctrine does not line up with our experience or tug on our emotional heart strings does not cast any doubt on its truthfulness.

Consider a few examples of thinkers who discard eternal judgment. First, William Neil argues that the doctrine of eternal judgment is unbiblical. He references those who embrace the "fire and brimstone school of theology, who revel in ideas such as that Christ was made a sacrifice to appease an angry God, or that the cross was a legal transaction in which an innocent victim was made to pay the penalty for the crimes of others, a propitiation of a stern God, find no support in Paul. These notions came into Christian theology by way of the legalistic minds of the medieval churchmen; they are not biblical Christianity."[104] Tragically, Neil's repudiation of the doctrine of eternal judgment has become the standard fare for many and appears to be growing in popularity.

Gerry Beauchemin holds that a belief in eternal judgment bears bad fruit and "compromises the Good News of the Gospel."[105] He maintains that hell is "unworthy of God. It strips Him of His glory, unlimited power, and unfailing love. It mars His holy and just character before all, depriving Him of the awesome worship He so deserves. It robs Christ of His victory over evil and dishonors His shed blood by limiting its power to save."[106] Beauchemin continues,

---

[104] William Neil, *Apostle Extraordinary* (London: Religious Education Press, 1965), 89-90. Cited in John R.W. Stott, *The Cross of Christ* (Downers Grove, Ill: InterVarsity, 1986), 172-173.

[105] Gerry Beauchemin, *Hope Beyond Hell: The Righteous Purpose of God's Judgment* (Olmito: Malista Press, 2007), 152.

[106] Ibid, 152-153.

"In truth, it destroys belief in One all-powerful GOD, and replaces Him with a pseudo-god who co-rules the earth with SATAN."[107] In his most recent book, Beauchemin adds, "Nothing dishonors God or fosters unbelief more than the horrid doctrine of endless punishment."[108]

Clark Pinnock stands alongside a growing number of Seminary professors who question the biblical doctrine of eternal punishment:

> *Everlasting torture is intolerable from a moral point of view because it pictures God acting like a bloodthirsty monster who maintains an everlasting Auschwitz for his enemies whom he does not allow to die. How can one love a God like that? I suppose one might be afraid of him, but could we love and respect him? Would we want to strive to be like him in such mercilessness?*[109]

In his book, *Love Wins,* Rob Bell is critical of a story we are all familiar with. This story, says Bell, is a "story about God who inflicts unrelenting punishment on people because they didn't do or say or believe the correct things in a brief window of time called life isn't a very good story."[110]

Is it possible that Bell is on target? Maybe this does not make for a good story after all. Here's the problem: *The story is true!* The Bible promises eternal life and the forgiveness of sins for all people who turn from their sinful rebellion and believe in, and follow, Christ (John 3:15-16; 6:37, 47; 7:38; John 8:12; Acts 4:12; Rom. 10:9-13, 17). And the Bible promises eternal judgment for the unrepentant; for those who refuse to believe in and obey Jesus (Deut. 32:40-41; 2 Thess. 1:8-9; Rom. 2:8). The apostle John adds, "Whoever believes in the Son has eternal life; whoever does not obey the Son shall not see life, but the wrath of God remains on him" (John 3:36). Therefore, we find that the story is not only true—the story is good! It is good because it is God's story.

---

[107] Ibid, 153.

[108] Gerry Beauchemin, *Hope for All: Ten Reasons God's Love Prevails* (Brownsville: Malista Press, 2018), 16.

[109] Clark Pinnock, "The Conditional View," *Four Views on Hell.* Ed. W.V. Crocket), 149. Secure more bibliographical data

[110] Rob Bell, *Love Wins: A Book About Heaven, Hell, and the Fate of Every Person Who Ever Lived* (New York: HarperCollins Publishers Inc., 2011), 110.

This story reminds us what we have been delivered from. It reminds unbelievers that God will punish sin and such a punishment is not only consistent with his holy character but is also integral to it. This good story reminds people everywhere that God has an intense hatred of sin. It reminds all people of the great length that God went to in order to vanquish the power and penalty of sin. Yet, many people who claim to "embrace Scripture," continue to discard the judgment of Christ.

THE SCRIPTURE DECLARES THAT GOD IS A GOD OF WRATH

Exodus 34:6-7 says, "The Lord passed before him and proclaimed, 'The Lord, the Lord, a God merciful and gracious, slow to anger, and abounding in steadfast love and faithfulness, keeping steadfast love for thousands, forgiving iniquity and transgression and sin, but who will by no means clear the guilty, visiting the iniquity of the fathers on the children and the children's children, to the third and the fourth generation.'" This passage tells us that God will "by no means clear the guilty." However, erosion has taken place in the church - and it has been happening over the last fifty years or so. Attributes of God such as love, mercy, and grace are elevated over attributes like justice and wrath. Over time, attributes like the wrath of God are eliminated altogether.

We must be careful to never minimize any of the attributes of God or "pit" attributes against each other. Wayne Grudem writes, "When Scripture speaks about God's attributes it never singles out one attribute of God as more important than all the rest. There is an assumption that every attribute is completely true of God and is true of all God's character."[111] Theologians refer to this as the *simplicity of God.* Grudem continues, "We must remember that God's *whole being* includes all of his attributes: he is entirely loving, entirely merciful, entirely just, and so forth. Every attribute of God that we find in Scripture is true of all of God's being, and we, therefore, can say that every attribute of God also qualifies every other attribute."[112] With this great reality in mind, let us turn our attention to the wrath of God.

---

[111] Wayne Grudem, *Systematic Theology* (Grand Rapids: Zondervan, 1994), 178.
[112] Ibid, 179.

DEFINING WRATH

In the New Testament, the Greek word *orgei* is translated as "anger, vengeance, fury, or indignation." It means "anger exhibited in punishment." John Stott defines wrath as "his steady, unrelenting, unremitting, uncompromising, antagonism to evil in all its forms and manifestations."[113] A.W. Tozer says, "The wrath of God is his eternal detestation of all unrighteousness ... It is the holiness of God stirred into activity against sin. It is the moving cause of that just sentence which he passes upon evildoers. God is angry against sin because it is a rebelling against his authority, a wrong done to his inviolable sovereignty."[114]

While many refuse to admit that God will exert his wrath on unrepentant people, Scripture speaks plainly about his almighty wrath. Notice a few examples:

> And the Lord said to Moses, "I have seen this people, and behold, it is a stiff-necked people. Now therefore let me alone, that my wrath may burn hot against them and I may consume them, in order that I may make a great nation of you" (Exod. 32:9–10).

> Remember and do not forget how you provoked the Lord your God to wrath in the wilderness. From the day you came out of the land of Egypt until you came to this place, you have been rebellious against the Lord. Even at Horeb you provoked the Lord to wrath, and the Lord was so angry with you that he was ready to destroy you (Deut. 9:7–8).

> Go, inquire of the Lord for me, and for the people, and for all Judah, concerning the words of this book that has been found. For great is the wrath of the Lord that is kindled against us, because our fathers have not obeyed the words of this book, to do according to all that is written concerning us (2 Kings 22:13).

---

[113] John R.W. Stott, *The Cross of Christ* (Downers Grove: InterVarsity Press, 1986), 173.
[114] A.W. Tozer, *The Attributes of God* (Grand Rapids: Baker Book House, 1975), 83.

For behold, the Lord will come in fire, and his chariots like the whirlwind, to render his anger in fury, and his rebuke with flames of fire. For by fire will the Lord enter into judgment, and by his sword, with all flesh; and those slain by the Lord shall be many (Isa. 66:15–16).

God's wrath is never capricious or impulsive. It is the righteous response of a holy God that burns hot against sin. John MacArthur identifies several different kinds of wrath:

- Cataclysmic wrath like the flood and the destruction of Sodom and Gomorrah.
- Consequential wrath - the law of sowing and reaping.
- Wrath of abandonment - removing restraint and letting people revel in their sin (Rom. 1).
- Eschatological wrath - the final Day of the Lord.
- Eternal wrath.[115]

DESCRIBING WRATH

When creatures violate the commands of God, he has a right to inflict punishment on the offender. The story of Uzzah reveals God's divine prerogative to display his holy wrath on disobedient creatures.

A Right to Wrath

First, *God has a right to wrath.* In 2 Samuel 6, we find the ark of God making its way to Jerusalem. The stipulations for transporting the ark have been meticulously recorded in Exodus 25:12-14. It is to be carried on the shoulders of the priests. Human hands are forbidden to touch the ark (Num. 4:15).

Despite the clear warnings, the ark was not transported in the way that God required—which made Uzzah culpable from the beginning. The oxen stumbled, which prompted Uzzah to reach out his hand in order to steady the ark and prevent it from touching the muddy ground. However, Uzzah failed to realize that his hand was as filthy as the mud that the ark was destined for. He failed to pay

---

[115] John MacArthur, *The MacArthur Study Bible* (Nashville: Word Books, 1997), 1993.

serious regard for the holiness of God and paid the ultimate price. 2 Samuel 6:7 records these sobering words: "And the anger of the LORD was kindled against Uzzah, and God struck him down there because of his error, and he died there beside the ark of God." A similar event unfolds in the book of Leviticus.

In Leviticus 10:1-3, we find the sons of Aaron offering unauthorized fire before the LORD:

> *Now Nadab and Abihu, the sons of Aaron, each took his censer and put fire in it and laid incense on it and offered unauthorized fire before the Lord, which he had not commanded them. And fire came out from before the Lord and consumed them, and they died before the Lord. Then Moses said to Aaron, "This is what the Lord has said: 'Among those who are near me I will be sanctified, and before all the people I will be glorified'" And Aaron held his peace (Lev. 10:1–3).*

Nadab and Abihu committed a serious and life-altering sin; a sin which cost them their lives. The New American Standard translation calls their offering "strange fire." The English Standard Version and the New International Version render the term, "unauthorized fire." The word comes from a Hebrew term which could also be translated as "illegitimate" or "illicit." Like Uzzah, Aaron's sons paid the ultimate sacrifice because they failed to regard God as holy.

A Reason to Exert Wrath

Second, *God always has a reason for exerting his wrath.* A.W. Pink comments, "Our readiness or our reluctance to meditate upon the wrath of God becomes a sure test of our hearts' attitude toward him. If we do not truly rejoice in God, for what he is in himself, and that because all the perfections which are eternally resident in him, then how dwelleth the love of God?"[116]

Robert Reymond continues:

> *God's wrath, of course, must not be construed in any measure as capricious, uncontrolled, or irrational fury. Nor is God himself malicious, vindictive, or spiteful. God's wrath is sim-*

---
[116] Pink, *The Attributes of God*, 85.

ply his instinctive holy indignation and the settled opposition of his holiness to sin, which, because he is righteous, expresses itself in judicial punishment.[117]

Notice several examples of God's wrath in the Old Testament:

God exerts his wrath on the Egyptians

Your right hand, O Lord, glorious in power, your right hand, O Lord, shatters the enemy. In the greatness of your majesty you overthrow your adversaries; you send out your fury; it consumes them like stubble (Exod. 15:6–7).

God exerts his wrath on the rebellious

And the people complained in the hearing of the Lord about their misfortunes, and when the Lord heard it, his anger was kindled, and the fire of the Lord burned among them and consumed some outlying parts of the camp (Num. 11:1).

God exerts his wrath on Judah

Still the Lord did not turn from the burning of his great wrath, by which his anger was kindled against Judah, because of all the provocations with which Manasseh had provoked him (2 Kings 23:26).

God exerts his wrath on his enemies

The Lord is a jealous and avenging God; the Lord is avenging and wrathful; the Lord takes vengeance on his adversaries and keeps wrath for his enemies. The Lord is slow to anger and great in power, and the Lord will by no means clear the guilty. His way is in whirlwind and storm, and the clouds are the dust of his feet. He rebukes the sea and makes it dry; he dries up all the rivers; Bashan and Carmel wither; the bloom of Lebanon withers. The mountains quake before him; the hills melt; the earth heaves before him, the world and all who

---

[117] Robert Reymond, *A New Systematic Theology of the Christian Faith* (Nashville: Thomas Nelson Publishers, 1998), 639.

dwell in it. Who can stand before his indignation? Who can endure the heat of his anger? His wrath is poured out like fire, and the rocks are broken into pieces by him (Nahum 1:1–6).

The wrath of God is also evident in the pages of the New Testament:

God exerts his wrath on people who suppress the truth about God

> *For the wrath of God is revealed from heaven against all ungodliness and unrighteousness of men, who by their unrighteousness suppress the truth. For what can be known about God is plain to them, because God has shown it to them (Rom. 1:18-19).*

> *But because of your hard and impenitent heart you are storing up wrath for yourself on the day of wrath when God's righteous judgment will be revealed (Rom. 2:5).*

God will exert his wrath on the unrepentant

> *But when he saw many of the Pharisees and Sadducees coming to his baptism, he said to them, "You brood of vipers! Who warned you to flee from the wrath to come?" (Matt. 3:7).*

God exerts his wrath on the disobedient

> *Put to death therefore what is earthly in you: sexual immorality, impurity, passion, evil desire, and covetousness, which is idolatry. On account of these the wrath of God is coming (Col. 3:5–6).*

God exerts his wrath on those who do not find their satisfaction in him

> *Whoever believes in the Son has eternal life; whoever does not obey the Son shall not see life, but the wrath of God remains on him (John 3:36).*

...He also will drink the wine of God's wrath, poured full strength into the cup of his anger, and he will be tormented with fire and sulfur in the presence of the holy angels and in the presence of the Lamb (Rev. 14:10).

Finally, *God decreed that his Son would drink the full expression of his wrath.* 2 Corinthians 5:21 says, *"For our sake he made him to be sin who knew no sin, so that in him we might become the righteousness of God."* The logic of the cross becomes evident when we begin to reflect on the Scripture and the purposes of God. Daniel Fuller summarizes the logic of the cross with four pivotal statements:[118]

God's righteousness consists in this—He has a love for his own glory.[119] Jonathan Edwards adds, "The moral rectitude of the disposition, inclination, or affection of God, chiefly consists in a regard to himself, infinitely above his regard to all other things; or, in other words, (God's) holiness consists in this (delighting to himself)."[120]

If God does everything for his own glory ... it follows that he will also take great pleasure in those who share this delight.[121]

God would not be loving to those who seek him if he did not vent the power of his wrath against those who remain unrepentant. Far from being in opposition to one another, God's love and wrath are simply two ways in which he makes it clear that he himself fully honors his name.[122]

If it can be shown that humanity has horribly sinned against God, then our sense of justice must call for a severe punishment, and the biblical teaching of eternal misery in hell for the unrepentant meets that requirement.[123]

---

[118] I am indebted to Daniel P. Fuller and Jonathan Edwards for their insight.
[119] Daniel Fuller, *The Unity of the Bible* (Grand Rapids: Zondervan Publishing House, 1992), 189.
[120] Jonathan Edwards, *Works,* 1:98. Cited in Ibid.
[121] Ibid, 189.
[122] Ibid.
[123] Ibid, 192.

What effect, then, should the doctrine of eternal punishment have on us? How does it change the way we live? How does it transform the way we think about the future?

First, *we should take sin seriously because God takes sin seriously.* Sin is not a "mere mistake" as some suppose. Sin is not a minor error or a lapse in judgment. The creeds and catechisms of the church help define the seriousness of sin. "Sin" as the Westminster Shorter Catechism notes, is "any want or conformity unto, or transgression of the law of God."[124] "Every sin, both original and actual, being a transgression of the righteous law of God, and contrary thereunto, doth, in its own nature, bring guilt upon the sinner, whereby he is bound over to the wrath of God, and curse of the law, and so made subject to death, with all miseries spiritual, temporal, and eternal."[125] *The Canons of Dort* add, "Since all men have sinned in Adam, lie under the curse, and are deserving of eternal death, God would have done no injustice by leaving them all to perish and delivering them over to condemnation on account of sin, according to the words of the apostle, 'that every mouth may be silenced and the whole world held accountable to God'" (Rom. 3:19).[126]

Second, *we should be motivated to share the gospel of grace with people who need the Savior.* When we consider the devastating effects of sin on the human race and the price that every unbeliever will pay for their sin, we should be motivated to action. The apostle Paul was prompted by God's Spirit as he considered people around him who were perishing without Christ: "I am speaking the truth in Christ—I am not lying; my conscience bears me witness in the Holy Spirit—that I have great sorrow and unceasing anguish in my heart. For I could wish that I myself were accursed and cut off from Christ for the sake of my brothers, my kinsmen according to the flesh" (Rom. 9:1–3). Paul had a heart for people. The gospel compelled him to minister to the needs of people around him. Paul understood that apart from the gospel, people would pay eternally for their sin.

---

[124] *Westminster Shorter Catechism* (Wheaton: Crossway Books, 2007), Kindle edition, Loc. 288.

[125] G.I. Williamson, Ed, *The Westminster Confession of Faith* (Phillipsburg: Presbyterian and Reformed, 2004), 77.

[126] *The Canons of Dort* (Winnipeg: Premier Printing LTD,1984), 532.

We too should be motivated to share the gospel of grace with people who need the Savior. No one is excluded - "for all have sinned and fall short of the glory of God" (Rom. 3:23). "For the love of Christ controls us, because we have concluded this: that one has died for all, therefore all have died" (2 Cor. 5:14). Since the love of Christ compels us, we share his great love with a world that is lost and hopeless apart from his gospel.

Third, *we should stand in humility because Jesus took the punishment we deserved.* Consider the great suffering that Jesus undertook both in his life and in his death. Hebrews 4:15 reminds us what our high priest endured: "For we do not have a high priest who is unable to sympathize with our weakness, but one who in every respect has been tempted as we are, yet without sin." And 1 Peter 2:24 reminds us of the active obedience of Jesus upon the cross: "He himself bore our sins in his body on the tree, that we might die to sin and live to righteousness. By his wounds you have been healed."

Jesus Christ bore the wrath of God on the cross. He endured 10,000 degrees of white-hot judgment. This is the judgment that each of us deserves. Yet Paul writes, "For our sake he made him to be sin who knew no sin, so that in him we might become the righteousness of God" (2 Cor. 5:21). Our only response to this selfless act of love is to bow in reverence to the sovereign king of the universe.

Fourth, *we should stand in humility because God gave us mercy.* Think of it: Instead of judging us eternally for our sins, God gave us mercy. "A clean conscience. A clean record. A clean heart. Free from accusation. Free from condemnation."[127] Instead of giving us what we deserved, the King of the universe determined to grant mercy to every person who trusts in Christ. The apostle Peter puts it like this: "Once you were not a people, but now you are God's people; once you had not received mercy, but now you have received mercy" (1 Peter 2:10).

Finally, *we should turn from our sin and turn to Christ alone for salvation.* The cross of Jesus Christ stands at the very center of human history. When we discard the judgment of Christ, we destroy

---

[127] Max Lucado, *Grace: More Than We Deserve, Greater Than We Imagine* (Nashville: Thomas Nelson, 2012), Kindle edition, 21.

the very essence of the gospel itself. Martin Lloyd-Jones observes the propensity of people to struggle in their search for joy—in large measure because they have failed to admit the consequences of sin:

> *If we adopt the modern philosophy and attitude of not believing in hell and in eternal punishment, and believe that, because God is love, everybody will somehow be all right in the end; if we believe that after death our souls are annihilated and go out of existence after a limited infliction of punishment which mercifully comes to an end, and that the whole thing is conditional—well, we must see that, as we detract in that way from our belief in the punishment of sin, so we are detracting from the good news of the gospel.*[128]

So, when we discard the judgment of Christ, we sacrifice much. We not only short-circuit our joy; we ignore the *white flag* flying high above the church.

---

[128] D. Martyn Lloyd-Jones, *Romans, Exposition of Chapter 1: The Gospel of God* (Carlisle: The Banner of Truth Trust, 1985), 59.

7

Demolishing the Christian Mind

———◆———

"We live in what may be the most anti-intellectual period in the history of Western civilization."

R.C. SPROUL

e have witnessed the compromised church and un-covered four areas in which doctrinal deceivers have gained headway into the household of faith. We have reflected briefly upon the *white flag* which has been unfurled in the open air and flies proudly for the world to see. In particular, we have seen:

- A dismantled God

- A disregarded doctrine

- A denigrated cross

- A discarded judgment

The final area we must consider is the Christian mind. To speak plainly, the Christian mind is deteriorating. The waves of secularism and religious pluralism pound relentlessly against the shore of the Christian mind, leading to a slow but steady erosion of biblical val-

— 97 —

ues. Make no mistake; a war is taking place and Christians are losing the battle. Fewer and fewer Christians are thinking Christianly in the twenty-first century. Sympathizers of postmodernism have exacerbated this problem by denying the existence of absolute truth, rejecting any ultimate source of truth, and ridiculing anyone who dares cling to a view of reality that is coherent, authoritative, and binds the conscience.

THE DECLINE OF THE CHRISTIAN MIND

The decline, descent, and the deterioration of the Christian mind is an undisputed reality. Francis Schaeffer warned the church about the erosion of the Christian mind in his classic work, *The God Who is There*. He specifically noted the seismic epistemological shift that was taking place: "The present chasm between the generations has been brought about almost entirely by a change in the concept of truth … The tragedy of our situation today is that men and women are being fundamentally affected by the new way of looking at truth, and yet they have never even analyzed the drift which has taken place."[129] Schaeffer observed that evangelicals in the '60s were failing to remember the importance of absolute truth. He added, "They took it for granted that if anything was true, the opposite was false. Absolutes imply antithesis … We must not forget that historic Christianity stands on the basis of antithesis. Without it, historic Christianity is meaningless. The basic antithesis is that God objectively exists in contrast (in antithesis) to his not existing."[130] Schaeffer's warning, for the most part, fell on deaf ears.

Harry Blamires agrees with Schaeffer's assessment: "We have manufactured a false 'charity' of the mind, which never takes a stand, but continually yields ground. It is proper to give way to people's interests: therefore it is proper to give way to other people's ideas. The damage done by this false deduction has been enormous."[131]

The church has slowly surrendered her call to develop the Christian mind and the damage continues to escalate. "The simple fact is that Sunday School as it's currently practiced is not doing the job of

---

[129] Francis A. Schaeffer, *The God Who is There* (Wheaton: Crossway Books, 1982), 5.
[130] Ibid, 6-8.
[131] Harry Blamires, *The Christian Mind* (Ann Arbor: Servant Publications, 1963), 39-40.

developing the Christian mind …"[132] The tragic result is subtle, deterioration of the Christian mind. Blamires laments, "There is no longer a Christian mind. It is commonplace that the mind of modern man has been secularized … But unfortunately, the Christian mind has succumbed to the secular drift with a degree of weakness and nervelessness unmatched in Christian history."[133] We find ourselves, then, in a situation that demands our immediate attention and a decisive resolve to educate and equip the Christian mind.

Apparently, rigorous thinking is not fashionable for some professing Christians in our generation. This non-sensical approach to the Christian life is counterproductive and ultimately plays into the hand of the enemy. J.C. Ryle offers this sobering warning for anyone who is attracted to the allure of a "feeling-centered" religion: "Believe me, this world is not a world in which we can do well without thinking, and least of all do well in the matter of our souls. 'Don't think,' whispers Satan. To their peril, many young men heed the devil and 'think no more.'"[134] Ryle's warning, of course, applies to young and old alike and is equally applicable to Christian men and women. Ignoring his advice leaves us weak and vulnerable. Ignoring his counsel contributes to the decline of the Christian mind.

DEFINING THE MIND

Before we go any further and discover how the mind is being disregarded and demolished in the church, we must first examine some of the finer points concerning the mind. This brief overview will help us discover some important biblical categories and determine the parameters before us.

Three important Greek words that describe the mind are included in the pages of the New Testament. The first and most common word is *nous,* translated "mind" or in a few cases as "understanding." The term points to the intellect and may point to reason in a narrower sense. It serves as the conduit for spiritual truth which has the

---

[132] J.P. Moreland, *Love Your God with All Your Mind* (Colorado Springs: NavPress, 1997), 196.

[133] Blamires, *The Christian Mind*, 3.

[134] J.C. Ryle, Cited in Douglas Bond, *Fathers and Sons: Stand Fast in the Way of Truth* (Phillipsburg: Presbyterian and Reformed, 2008), 29.

capacity to recognize good and evil. Passages describing *nous* include the following:

> *You were taught, with regard to your former way of life, to put off your old self, which is being corrupted by its deceitful desires; to be made new in the attitude of your minds (nous); and to put on the new self, created to be like God in true righteousness and holiness (Eph. 4:22–24, NIV).*

> *Now this I say and testify in the Lord, that you must no longer walk as the Gentiles do, in the futility of their minds (nous) (Eph. 4:17).*

> *And the peace of God, which surpasses all understanding, will guard your hearts and your minds (nous) in Christ Jesus (Phil. 4:7).*

An important principle emerges in these passages, namely, we are instructed to be made new in the attitude of our minds. We must not only think Christianly; we must act Christianly. Herein lies the key: *Christian thinking precedes Christian action.* A Christian response that does not include Christian thinking is a contradiction. Indeed, a proper Christian response is grounded in the truth. For example, a qualified physician needs the facts before operating. Any doctor who dares to perform surgery apart from the facts demonstrates not only a lack of good judgment but also makes a mockery out of the profession. An athlete needs to master the basics in order to be successful in a given sport. Knowledge always precedes a proper response.

The second Greek term, *phroneō,* is translated, "think," or "regard." It suggests the direction of one's mind; what one seeks after or strives for. Notice several passages of Scripture in which the term appears:

> *Set your minds (phroneō) on things that are above, not on things that are on earth (Col. 3:2).*

> *For those who live according to the flesh set their minds (phroneō) on the things of the flesh, but those who live according to the Spirit set their minds on the things of the Spirit (Rom. 8:5).*

*Their end is destruction, their god is their belly, and they glory
in their shame, with minds (phroneō) set on earthly things.
But our citizenship is in heaven, and from it we await a Savior,
the Lord Jesus Christ ... (Phil. 3:19–20).*

Another principle may be drawn from these texts and relates
directly to the development of the Christian mind. We are instructed to set our minds on things above; to specifically set our minds
on things of the Spirit and live according to the divine standard set
forth in the Word of God. Our minds must be devoted exclusively to
God and his precepts. The only alternative is devotion to the world,
the flesh, and the devil whose ultimate end reaps eternal destruction.

Finally, notice the Greek word, *logizomai,* which is translated
"think," "impute," "reckon," or "reason." The word literally means,
"to weigh the reasons," or "to deliberate." This word deals with reality. *Logizomai* refers to facts, not mere suppositions. A few passages
which describe this term are as follows:

*When I was a child, I spoke like a child, I thought like a child,
I reasoned (logizomai) like a child. When I became a man, I
gave up childish ways (1 Cor. 13:11).*

*Finally, brothers, whatever is true, whatever is honorable,
whatever is just, whatever is pure, whatever is lovely, whatever is commendable, if there is any excellence, if there is anything worthy of praise, think (logizomai) about these things
(Phil. 4:8).*

So thinking Christianly involves thinking God's thoughts after
him. Focusing on truth brings glory to God. Clearly, this is a remind-
er that the Christian mind must be nurtured and developed with
great patience and discipline. The Christian mind must be shaped by
the dictates of Scripture rather than the lure of postmodern culture.
In short, "the mind of man" writes Harry Blamires, "must be won
for God."[135] Anything less is disobedient to Scripture and represents
a turning away from God and his truth.

---

[135] Blamires, *The Christian Mind,* 81.

DEMOLISHING THE MIND

Tragically, the Christian mind is being downplayed and as a result, is deteriorating. Our task in this chapter is to narrow our focus on the rampant anti-intellectualism that has invaded the church.

Anti-Intellectualism

I personally heard R.C. Sproul lament the deplorable condition of the Christian mind on several occasions. Sproul said, "We live in what may be the most anti-intellectual period in the history of Western civilization."[136] There is an unhealthy bias in the church against anything that is intellectually rigorous or academically challenging. For many men, pastoral ministry is a steep uphill climb that militates against a watered-down version of the Christian faith. Instead of the Puritans, people want something palatable. Instead of challenging doctrine, the church clamors for crumbs. Large segments of the church are content with milk when they should be striving for spiritual meat (1 Pet. 2:2-3).

This is not a new trend. For years, the church has been plagued by this anti-intellectual bent. Surprisingly, the well-known pastor, D.L. Moody was critical of theology. When someone inquired about his theology, he replied, "My theology! I didn't know I had any. I wish you would tell me what my theology is."[137]

John Piper confronts this anti-intellectualism in his excellent book, *Think: The Life of the Mind and the Love of God*. The aim of the book "is to encourage serious, faithful, humble thinking that leads to the true knowledge of God, which leads to loving him, which overflows in loving others."[138] Piper is advocating scrupulous thinking which is radically Christian. Such a commitment necessarily leads to radical, Christ-saturated living where people are touched by the magnanimous hope, claims, and promises of the gospel.

The growing anti-intellectual instinct among evangelicals is troubling, especially in light of the biblical references that insist

---

[136] R.C. Sproul, Cited in John Piper, *Think: The Life of the Mind and the Love of God* (Wheaton: Crossway, 2010), 29.

[137] D.L. Moody, cited in John Piper, *Think: The Life of the Mind and the Love of God* (Wheaton: Crossway Books, 2010), 122.

[138] Ibid, 154.

something entirely different. Paul calls us to a life of constant mind renewal: "Do not be conformed to this world, but be transformed by the renewal of your mind, that by testing you may discern what is the will of God, what is good and acceptable and perfect" (Rom. 12:2). Our minds are to be daily transformed by the truth of God's revealed Word, his written truth.

The people of God are called to be consumed by God's truth and controlled by God's truth. Colossians 1:9-10 says, "And so, from the day we heard, we have not ceased to pray for you, asking that you may be filled with the knowledge of his will in all spiritual wisdom and understanding, so as to walk in a manner worthy of the Lord, fully pleasing to him, bearing fruit in every good work and increasing in the knowledge of God." Anything that falls short of God's divine standard is tantamount to compromise and waters down the mandate to be consumed and controlled by divine truth.

We are called to be truth-centered Christians who are filled with a knowledge of God's will. The term *filled* (*pleiróō*) means "to fill to the top; to accomplish; to bring to full realization; to be totally controlled." The meaning of this term is best seen in a few New Testament passages:

> *These things I have spoken to you, that my joy may be in you, and that your joy may be* **full (pleiróō)** *(John 15:11).*

> *Again, the kingdom of heaven is like a net that was thrown into the sea and gathered fish of every kind. When it was* **full (pleiróō)**, *men drew it ashore and sat down and sorted the good into containers but threw away the bad (Matt. 13:47–48).*

> *Mary therefore took a pound of expensive ointment made from pure nard, and anointed the feet of Jesus and wiped his feet with her hair. The house was* **filled (pleiróō)** *with the fragrance of the perfume (John 12:3).*

However, Colossians 1 is not referring to a net which is full of fish or a room filled with perfume. The passage is referring to a Christian who is overflowing with a knowledge of God's will. "Knowledge" (*èpignōsis*) is a precise knowledge; a knowledge that is full and rich and deep. This is a combination of head and heart knowledge. This "knowledge" is in sharp contrast to what the Gnostics were advocating in the first century, in which doctrine and rationality are discarded and replaced with so-called "secret knowledge."

Examples of *knowledge* (*èpignōsis*) are found through the pages of the New Testament:

> ...*to equip the saints for the work of ministry, for building up the body of Christ, until we all attain to the unity of the faith and of the* **knowledge** (*èpignōsis*) *of the Son of God, to mature manhood, to the measure of the stature of the fullness of Christ* ... (*Eph. 4:12–13*).

> *And it is my prayer that your love may abound more and more, with* **knowledge** (*èpignōsis*) *and all discernment* ... (*Phil. 1:9*).

> *Paul, a servant of God and an apostle of Jesus Christ, for the sake of the faith of God's elect and their* **knowledge** (*èpignōsis*) *of the truth, which accords with godliness* ... (*Titus 1:1*).

To downplay or denigrate knowledge in the Christian life is like planting a garden and refusing to water it. Yet the general pattern of Christian discipleship in our culture is geared toward feelings and subjectivism. Experiencing God has replaced the mandate to know him. Walk into a Christian bookstore and ask where the theology section is located. The typical response will be a blank stare. Or at best, you may encounter a well-meaning person who says, "We have a few theology books in the back of the store."

In many ways, we have returned to the days of pietism. Mark Noll describes this movement as "a recurring tendency within Christian history to emphasize more practicalities of Christian life and less the formal structures of theology ..."[139] Pastors who emphasize systematic and biblical theology will inevitably face the pernicious influence of pietism and must be prepared to stand strong in a culture awash in experimentalism.

---

[139] Mark Noll, Cited in Walter Elwell, Ed. *The Evangelical Dictionary of Theology* (Grand Rapids: Baker Book House, 1984), 855.

Additionally, downplaying the "knowledge" component of the Christian life is deadly to the sanctification process:

Desire without knowledge is not good, and whoever makes haste with his feet misses his way (Prov. 19:2).

Therefore my people go into exile for lack of knowledge; their honored men go hungry, and their multitude is parched with thirst (Isa. 5:13).

My people are destroyed for lack of knowledge; because you have rejected knowledge ... (Hosea 4:6).

The truth-centered Christian understands the importance of applying the Word of God to daily living. Paul's desire is that we might be filled with the knowledge of God's will "in all spiritual wisdom and understanding" (Col. 1:9b) which refers to the integration and application of spiritual truth to daily situations. We are to take what we "know" and apply that knowledge directly to our daily lives. We apply biblical principles to our families and the workplace. Indeed, we apply God's principles to the whole of life.

Paul not only prays for us to be consumed by the truth, he prays for our lives to be transformed. The principle is clear: When truth consumes us, that same truth transforms us! Growing in Christ never takes place in a vacuum. Rather, we see a pattern of truth lovers who are transformed for God's glory.

A transformed life bears the progressive marks of the Holy Spirit's work. Paul refers to such a person as one who walks in a "manner worthy of the Lord, fully pleasing to him, bearing fruit in every good work and increasing in the knowledge of God" (Col. 1:10). And so what are the marks of a believer who bears the marks of ongoing transformation? First, we are called to a *worthy walk*. The worthy walk describes the way in which a man or a woman conduct his or her life. This worthy walk is an important New Testament theme. Scripture refers to people who:

- Walk in newness of life (Rom. 6:4).
- Walk honestly (Rom. 13:13).

- Walk by faith (2 Cor. 5:7).
- Walk in the Spirit (Gal. 5:16).
- Walk in love (Eph. 5:2).
- Walk as children of the light (Eph. 5:8).
- Walk circumspectly (Eph. 5:15).
- Walk in truth (2 John 1:4).
- Walk worthily (Eph. 4:1; 1 Thess. 2:12).

Second, we are called to lives which *bear fruit*. Colossians 1:10 specifically says that we are to bear fruit "in every good work." Jesus says, "I am the vine; you are the branches. Whoever abides in me and I in him, he it is that bears much fruit, for apart from me you can do nothing" (John 15:5). He adds, "By this my Father is glorified, that you bear much fruit and so prove to be my disciples" (John 15:8). And Paul observes that fruit-bearing in the lives of believers was appointed in eternity past: "For we are his workmanship, created in Christ Jesus for good works, which God prepared beforehand, that we should walk in them" (Eph. 2:10).

Third, we are called to *increase in the knowledge of God.* The Greek term translated *increase* means "to grow or augment." That is, we are to give constant attention to growing in our knowledge of God. Once again, we see the indispensable need for a strong theological infrastructure in our lives. We must commit ourselves to studying theology. Our lives should be devoted to learning everything about God until our final breath. Calvin affirms, "We must always make progress in the doctrine of godliness until death."[140] Our progress must be an ongoing process, all the way to the shores of the Celestial City.

Fourth, we are called to be people of *spiritual strength.* Paul writes, "May you be strengthened with all power, according to his glorious might, for all endurance and patience with joy …" (Col. 1:11). *Strengthened* means "powerful, strong, or competent." Matthew Henry adds, "To be strengthened is to be furnished by the grace of God for every good work, and fortified by that grace against ev-

---

[140] John Calvin, *Galatians, Philippians and Colossians* (Grand Rapids: Eerdmans Publishing Company, 1965), 305.

ery evil."[141] This spiritual strength finds its origin in God's glorious might. The Puritan divine adds, "The grace of God in the hearts of believers is the power of God; and there is a glory in this power."[142] But notice the unbelievable aspects of this spiritual strength in verse 11: This spiritual strength is "for all endurance and patience with joy …" Such spiritual strength marks the faithful follower of Christ in this generation.

Finally, we are called to be a *thankful people*. "… Giving thanks to the Father, who has qualified you to share in the inheritance of the saints in light." A thankful heart is a defining quality of a mature Christian. This is a repeated theme in the pages of the New Testament:

> *Rejoice always, pray without ceasing, give thanks in all circumstances; for this is the will of God in Christ Jesus for you (1 Thess. 5:16–18).*

> *And let the peace of Christ rule in your hearts, to which indeed you were called in one body. And be thankful. Let the word of Christ dwell in you richly, teaching and admonishing one another in all wisdom, singing psalms and hymns and spiritual songs, with thankfulness in your hearts to God. And whatever you do, in word or deed, do everything in the name of the Lord Jesus, giving thanks to God the Father through him (Col. 3:15–17).*

> *Continue steadfastly in prayer, being watchful in it with thanksgiving (Col. 4:2).*

The rampant anti-intellectualism which has invaded the church is a troubling development, indeed. It is yet another sign of the compromised church. It is a clear indication that the *white flag* continues to gain momentum to the utter shame and disgrace of the church.

FIGHTING VALIANTLY FOR THE CAUSE OF TRUTH

Tragically, we in the twenty-first-century church are not the first to face intense challenges and battle compromise. Many courageous

---

[141] Matthew Henry, *The Matthew Henry Commentary* (Grand Rapids: Zondervan Publishing House, 1992), 683.
[142] Ibid.

Christians have maintained their allegiance to God and his Word. The heroes of church history fought valiantly for the cause of truth. These faithful people pursued God with passion and served people with humility and unrelenting resolve. The Word of God was their highest authority and the gospel of Jesus Christ was their never-ending passion. Two men, in particular, stand out as we consider such courage in the face of adversity.

Athanasius

Athanasius lived in an age in which the *white flag* of compromise flew with shameful abandon. The well-known African bishop served his Lord for forty-five years. Seventeen of those years were spent in the shadows as he was exiled for his faithful proclamation of the gospel and staunch defense of orthodoxy, including a rigorous battle he waged over the deity of Christ and his repudiation of the Arian heresy.

When the world around him departed from the faith, Athanasius stood strong. When the world compromised, Athanasius stood courageously. When the world jettisoned the faith, Athanasius clung to the faith with all his might. When the world discarded the truth, the African bishop demanded faithfulness to the truth. This stalwart of the Christian faith stood *contra mundum,* "against the world." John Piper adds, "He stood steadfast against overwhelming defection from orthodoxy, and only at the end of his life could he see the dawn of triumph."[143] Compromise, for Athanasius, was tantamount to defection from historic Christianity. Compromise was simply an unacceptable word in his vocabulary.

Like many heroes of the Christian faith, Athanasius lived a risky life. His rigid stand for the cause of truth often left him hanging precariously from the cliff of controversy. Piper observes, "It is one of the typical ironies of God's providence that the triumph over Arianism would happen largely through the ministry of a fugitive living and writing within inches of his death."[144] It is this kind of steely resolve that is needed in the twenty-first-century church. This kind of courage should mark every follower of the Lord Jesus Christ.

---

[143] John Piper, *Contending for Our All* (Wheaton: Crossway Books, 2006), 41.
[144] Ibid, 55.

Charles Haddon Spurgeon

C.H. Spurgeon is another example of a man who valiantly fought
for the cause of truth. He courageously battled liberalism and stood
strong against the hyper-Calvinists of the day. He maintained his
integrity when his character was falsely maligned. He opposed doctrinal deceivers and resisted denominational frauds. And he held fast
to the authority of Scripture, even when the shifting sands of compromise beckoned him to crumble. Like Athanasius, the Prince of
Preachers was never content to merely accept the status quo. For
Spurgeon, controversy was a normal part of everyday ministry.

> *Controversy is never a very happy element for the child of
> God: he would far rather be in communion with his Lord
> than be engaged in defending the faith, or in attacking er-
> ror. But the soldier of Christ knows no choice in his Master's
> commands. He may feel it to be better for him to lie upon
> the bed of rest than to stand covered with the sweat and
> dust of battle; but, as a soldier, he has learned to obey, and
> the rule of his obedience is not his personal comfort, but his
> Lord's absolute command. The servant of God must endeav-
> or to maintain all the truth which his Master has revealed
> to him, because as a Christian soldier, this is part of his duty.
> But while he does so, he accords to others the liberty which
> he himself enjoys.* [145]

The faithful preacher from London understood that compromise
was simply unacceptable in the church. So, he fought courageously
for the cause of truth. Spurgeon refused to back down. He made his
mark. He never surrendered. Each sermon bore the indelible marks
of the cross and pled with sinners to find refuge in the Savior who
bore the sin of every person who would ever believe.

Athanasius and Spurgeon were men of principle; they were men
of theological valor; they were men who were utterly unwilling to
waver on the truth. They were men who truly stood *contra mundum,*
"against the world." These godly men serve as role models for our

[145] C.H. Spurgeon, *Autobiography, Volume 2: Full Harvest* (Edinburgh: The Banner
of Truth Trust, 1973), 468.

generation and inspire us to fight valiantly for the cause of truth, the gospel of Christ, and the glory of God!

In Part One, we considered the *challenged church*. In so doing, we confronted and discerned the spirit of the age. We discovered a *white flag* that reveals a deadly deal which has been struck with the world.

In Part Two, we examined the compromised church. We witnessed the horrible effects of a God who has been dismantled and doctrine that has been disregarded. We have seen how Christ's work has been denigrated and how the judgment of Christ has been discarded. We are eye-witnesses to the demolition of the Christian mind.

We have only scratched the surface in our discussion of the five areas of compromise. There are many other areas where the *white flag* is flying in the local church. For instance, the *white flag* is manifested in a blatant disregard for gender roles in the so-called egalitarian movement. The *white flag* is revealed in a widespread acceptance of "same-sex marriage." And the *white flag* is displayed in many churches who pay no regard to the authority of Scripture.

In Part Three, *the call to the church,* we will take an offensive stance. We will respond to the compromised church and offer a series of biblical challenges. These challenges provide a template for Christ-followers to move forward with obedience to the Lord. While the challenges and the threat of compromise may shift from one generation to the next, the *call* to the church is the same throughout redemptive history. The church (*ekklesia*) includes the people of God who have been *called out*. The church is the *"pillar and buttress of the truth"* (1 Tim. 3:15).

Like Athanasius and Spurgeon, we are called to stand tall and firm for the sake of Christ. Such a stance will prove to be unpopular. However, standing firm as a Christian has never been a popular move. Indeed, standing firm and boldly proclaiming the truth is a counter-cultural endeavor which will be met with stiff resistance and persecution.

So we are called to stand *contra mundum,* which is one of the marks of a faithful Christian. Anything less than total surrender to Christ is untenable and unacceptable. Anything less than absolute devotion to the kingdom priorities of Jesus is intolerable. So we march forward and remain true to our call. This is the *call to the church* and the focus of the remainder of the book.

PART THREE:

THE CALL TO THE CHURCH

<hr/>

"My concluding sentence is simply this: The world is lost, the God of the Bible does exist; the world is lost, but truth is truth. Keep on! And for how long? I'll tell you. Keep on, keep on, keep on, keep on, and then KEEP ON!"[146]

---

[146] Francis A. Schaeffer, *Death in the City* (Wheaton: Crossway Books, reprint 1982), 256.

8

A Strategic Posture

"*Never give in—never, never, never, never, in nothing great or small, large or petty, never give in except to convictions of honor and good sense. Never yield to force; never yield to the apparently overwhelming might of the enemy.*"

WINSTON CHURCHILL

S trategy is a crucial aspect of every coach, chief executive, leader, or pastor. Effective strategy enables leaders to see the big picture. It enables them to gain the necessary perspective as they move forward and advance in the direction of the targeted initiatives of their team or organization. The local church is no different. Pastors and elders must help people see the big picture. They must develop strategic initiatives to move toward the fulfillment of stated goals. They must faithfully guide the flock, steering clear of compromise, and carefully lead those entrusted to their care.

As we face the *white flag of compromise*, it is vital that we develop a strategy in the coming days. What will our commitments be as followers of Jesus? What are the non-negotiable components of our worldview? Four critical components will serve as the basis for our initial strategy. Once this biblical strategy is in place, we will be in a position to present a posture in the concluding chapters, which is both offensive and vigilant.

STAND FIRM

The first component of our strategy is to *stand firm*. The Greek word translated *stand* means to "persevere, remain, or abide." 1 Corinthians 15:58 makes this point plain: "Therefore, my beloved brothers, be steadfast, immovable, always abounding in the work of the Lord, knowing that in the Lord your labor is not in vain." The call to be *steadfast* comes from a Greek word that means "to be firm," especially in the area of convictions. If we plan on confronting *the white flag* with any amount of effectiveness, we must stand firm, that is, we must hold steadfast convictions.

These convictions are *doctrinal convictions*. God calls us to maintain our commitment to the clear doctrinal standards of Scripture. Paul instructed Timothy to keep a close watch on "the teaching" or doctrine. We are called upon to guard Christian truth like a treasure chest, which is filled with precious pearls. The psalmist proclaims:

> *The law of the Lord is perfect, reviving the soul; the testimony of the Lord is sure, making wise the simple; the precepts of the Lord are right, rejoicing the heart; the commandment of the Lord is pure, enlightening the eyes; the fear of the Lord is clean, enduring forever; the rules of the Lord are true, and righteous altogether. More to be desired are they than gold, even much fine gold; sweeter also than honey and drippings of the honeycomb (Ps. 19:7–10).*

The doctrinal truths in Scripture are precious realities which must be treasured and protected. Therefore, we must cling tenaciously to these precious jewels. We must stand firm! But such a stance requires courage and steadfastness. John MacArthur highlights the importance of maintaining strong doctrinal convictions: "Now is not a good time for Christians to flirt with the spirit of the age. We cannot afford to be apathetic about the truth God has put in our trust. It is our duty to guard, proclaim, and pass on that truth to the next generation."[147] We must stand fast in our doctrinal convictions.

---

[147] John F. MacArthur, *The Truth War: Fighting for Certainty in an Age of Deception*, 23.

These convictions are *moral convictions*. Such convictions inform our responses to hot topics such as same-sex marriage, abortion, the legalization of marijuana, physician assisted suicide, and the like. Unfortunately, the moral convictions of most people are either non-existent or eroding. Most troubling are the eroding moral convictions in the church. Many Christians have been sucked in unknowingly by the lure of moral relativism which renders them spineless and ineffective. So as the *white flag* rises, the people of God stand by passively and allow the dictates of the deceived to blow them into a godless wasteland.

As I write at a local coffee shop, a worker outside is blowing the sidewalk debris with a high-powered machine. Customers and employees at the coffee shop are standing in awe as pollen rises from the ground and mimics a virtual snowstorm in the month of May. It is a strange sight to see the nefarious pollen floating freely in the air. I am struck by the bewildered people standing with their faces pressed against the window. We are alarmed by a cloud of pollen, which at worst, may lead to a day filled with sniffles or an allergic reaction. Yet the church stands in utter disregard when the *white flag of compromise* flies proudly above our heads. Our minds and hearts have grown ice-cold and apathetic in the face of apostasy.

But the Word of God calls us to be staunch and devoted, even in the midst of compromise. We are not only called to be steadfast; we are also called to be "immovable" according to 1 Corinthians 15:58. An immoveable person is unshaken or steady, ready and willing to serve the Lord. When we make a commitment to be immoveable, we make a mental commitment to hold our ground. We make a commitment to stand strong against the musings of postmodernity and cling to the rock-solid truths of Scripture. There is no vacillation for the immovable person. Compromise is not a part of this person's vocabulary. The immoveable person draws clear lines, has strong convictions, and stands steady, even when the winds of false teaching threaten his very existence.

Notice the result of the person who is steadfast and immoveable. This person is a fruitful member of God's kingdom, "abounding in the work of the Lord" (1 Cor. 15:58). The efforts of this person are not in vain. Thus, the people of God benefit mightily from this kind of obedience. And God is greatly glorified as the people of God make their stand in an ungodly world.

Os Guinness reminds us that "the Greek word for resurrection (*anastasis*) literally means 'a standing up again.'"[148] The author continues:

> Despite everyone and despite everything, we are called to stand, and stand we must as God's impossible people. However sweet the seduction, however popular and powerful the tide, however plausible the different gospel, however scornful or brutal the attacks, and however fearful the threats, impossible people stand, faithful only to Jesus, our Lord and our God. So may it be in our time.[149]

The first strategic initiative is to *stand firm* strong in a culture which is dominated by the shifting winds of compromise. When the *white flag* is hoisted high in the air, we choose to stand firm. Instead of being "tossed to and fro by the waves and carried about by every wind of doctrine" (Eph. 4:14), we choose to stand strong and maintain our allegiance to our Sovereign King. We stand strong in our convictions. We stand strong in our confidence in Scripture. We choose to stand firm in the faith.

RECLAIM OUR IDENTITY

Another strategic initiative is to *reclaim our identity*. Make no mistake: We have everything we need in Christ. We have the full measure of Christ. We have been filled with Christ who is fully God and rules with majestic sovereignty. Yet, there is a definite identity crisis in the church today. Some evangelicals have clearly lost their way. They have strayed off the path; they have compromised the truth. Some Christians have not only forgotten that they are complete in Christ, they have forgotten their identity all-together.

The symptoms of this "evangelical identity crisis" are clear. We live in an age of rampant unconfessed sin. When people actually

---

[148] Os Guinness, *Impossible People: Christian Courage and the Struggle for the Soul of Civilization,* Kindle edition, Loc. 3030.
[149] Ibid.

admit and confess their sin, many refuse to repent of their sin. There is a reckless disregard for the lordship of Christ and the holiness of God. A cavalier attitude is running rampant in the church and is tarnishing the bride. To be candid, we have forgotten who we are in Christ.

People flock to the latest seminar to improve their self-worth. Others seek advice from self-help authors who import practices from the secular marketplace like self-actualization, visualization, etc. Unsatisfied with their lot in life, some people run to the latest televangelist to find the latest and greatest "formula for success." Some turn to pop psychology, philosophy, or sociology for answers. Evangelicals are purchasing books that may give Christ "lip-service" but fail to promote the birthright that every believer should enjoy. Why do self-help books fly off the shelves in bookstores? The simple answer is that many people fail to remember who they truly are in Christ. They have a great interest in self-worth but have forgotten the supreme worth of God.

Who are we as Christ-followers? As people who are complete in Christ, what exactly is our identity? The Scripture clearly teaches this fundamental reality: *We were buried with Christ in baptism and we were raised with Christ so that we might live new lives to the glory of God.*

We Were Buried with Christ in Baptism

Scripture proclaims, "In him also you were circumcised with a circumcision made without hands, by putting off the body of the flesh, by the circumcision of Christ, having been buried with him in baptism, in which you were also raised with him through faith in the powerful working of God, who raised him from the dead" (Col. 2:11–12). This astonishing reality was accomplished in the past. This reality was accomplished by the Holy Spirit. This reality was a sovereign act of the Holy Spirit. Scripture says, "For in one Spirit we were all baptized into one body—Jews or Greeks, slaves or free—and all were made to drink of one Spirit" (1 Cor. 12:13).

First, *we were buried with him in baptism*. The term *buried* means "to identify with Christ in his death." Paul makes this point clear:

For as many of you as were baptized into Christ have put on Christ (Gal.3:27).

Do you not know that all of us who have been baptized into Christ Jesus were baptized into his death? We were buried therefore with him by baptism into death, in order that, just as Christ was raised from the dead by the glory of the Father, we too might walk in newness of life (Rom. 6:3–4).

To be buried with Christ, then, is to be united with Christ. "Apart from union with Christ," writes John Murray, "we cannot view past, present, or future with anything but dismay and Christless dread … Union with Christ binds all together and ensures that to all for whom Christ has purchased redemption he effectively applies and communicates the same."[150]

Second, *we have been baptized into his death.* That is, we are "in" Christ. The apostle Paul echoes this great reality in two breathtaking passages:

There is therefore now no condemnation for those who are in Christ Jesus. For the law of the Spirit of life has set you free in Christ Jesus from the law of sin and death (Rom. 8:1-2).

Therefore, if anyone is in Christ, he is a new creation. The old has passed away; behold, the new has come (2 Cor. 5:17).

The Greek word for baptism is *baptidzō,* a term that means "to dip, immerse, or submerge." When a white cloth is introduced to a bath infused with food coloring, the condition of the cloth changes. It becomes *united* with a different environment. LLoyd-Jones remarks, "So it is true to say of us that, as a man when he dies and is buried has entirely finished with this realm and life in which we live, so when we were buried with Christ it was the final proof of the fact that we also have finished the reign and the realm and the rule of the power of sin."[151]

This is precisely what baptism by immersion seeks to illustrate. When a baptismal candidate is *dipped* into the water, it demonstrates

---

[150] John Murray, *Redemption Accomplished and Applied* (Grand Rapids: Eerdmans Publishing Company, 1955), 165.

[151] Martin Lloyd-Jones, *Romans: The New Man* (Carlisle: The Banner of Truth, 1972), 47.

what took place when he or she was buried with Christ in baptism. Every person who trusts in Christ's completed work on the cross is buried with Christ in baptism.

Notice four practical points of application. First, *since we are no longer under the reign of sin, this tyrant no longer controls our lives.* Before we followed Jesus, we were dominated by the reign of sin. We were under the rulership of sin. We were under the dictatorship of sin's tyrannical grip.

You may remember when Saddam Hussein dominated the nation of Iraq. He controlled people. He ruled them with an iron fist. The people were under his reign—and oh, was it a brutal reign. But there came a day when Saddam was captured and eventually sentenced for his crimes and marched to the gallows. No longer would he rule and reign over the people of Iraq. He was gone forever! So it is for the believer in Jesus Christ. The reign of sin has been defeated. This brutal tyrant no longer controls our lives.

Second, *since we are no longer under the reign of sin, we are no longer slaves to sin.* In John 8:34-35, Jesus clearly articulates this principle: "Truly, truly, I say to you, everyone who commits sin is a slave to sin. The slave does not remain in the house forever; the son remains forever. So if the Son sets you free, you will be free indeed." The power of sin no longer rules in our lives. We have been set free by the Lord Jesus Christ.

Third, *since we are no longer under the reign of sin, we are under a new domain—the reign of grace.* "For sin will have no dominion over you, since you are not under law but under grace" (Rom. 6:14). Our old master has been defeated. Our lives as Christians are under a new jurisdiction. We are subject to Jesus and his sovereign lordship.

Fourth, *when we do commit sin, it is because we have failed to realize who we are in Christ.* It is at this point, we fall prey to the evangelical identity crisis. We fail to live up to our high calling as Christians.

We Were Raised with Christ

Not only were we buried with Christ in baptism, we were raised with Christ (Col. 2:12). This amazing reality was also accomplished in the past. This reality was a sovereign act of God. Paul sounds this triumphant note in his letter to the Romans: "We were buried therefore with him by baptism into death, in order that, just as Christ was raised from the dead by the glory of the Father, we too might walk in newness of life. For if we have been united with him in a death like his, we shall certainly be united with him in a resurrection like his" (Romans 6:4–5). We were raised with him through the instrument of faith—faith in the powerful working of God, who raised Jesus from the dead. "With this exceeding great power to 'us-ward that believe,' with this power of the resurrection already working in us, the vanquished rule and reign of sin can never possess us again."[152] The same power that raised Christ from the dead is operating in us!

When a baptismal candidate emerges from the water, we remember this glorious truth - they have been raised with Christ! *We were buried with Christ in baptism, and we were raised with Christ so that we might live a new life to the glory of God.*

Our identity, therefore, must be wrapped up exclusively in Christ. He is the One who paid the price for sinners and provides an indelible passport to heaven for anyone who repents of their sins and trusts in him.

PERSEVERE

Our strategic posture involves *standing firm* and *reclaiming our identity*. But the final strategic posture involves *perseverance*. I have many friends who have fought valiantly against cancer. With bold resolve and determination, these godly men and women faced this deadly disease with courage and God-centered strength. When the *white flag* flies menacingly above the church, we too must persevere.

Jude was a servant of the Lord Jesus and the brother of James. He encouraged believers to "contend for the faith that was once for all delivered to the saints" (Jude 3). False teachers had invaded the first-century church. Like today, the *white flag* was having its way among the people of God. So Jude described these false teachers throughout his letter. He painted a rather brutal portrait of these trouble-makers and describes them as:

---

[152] Ibid, 54.

- Ungodly
- Rebelling against God
- Fault-finding
- Grumbling
- Turning grace into license
- Resisting spiritual authority
- Selfish
- Proud
- Twisting God's grace

Additionally, Jude issues a five-fold warning against these apostates. They are mockers, following ungodly lusts, divisive, worldly-minded, and devoid of the Spirit.

A shift, however, takes place in Jude's letter in verse 20. The remaining words of his little letter are devoted to encouraging the people of God. He offers wisdom to Christ-followers and provides a powerful prescription for them to persevere in light of the wolves who threaten to undermine their faith. Jude's message is as relevant for us today as it was in the first-century church.

The prescription for perseverance is a commitment to developing spiritual muscles, depending on the Holy Spirit, desiring God above all, and demonstrating the compassion of Christ to people.

Develop Our Spiritual Muscles

Jude challenges Christ-followers to lay a proper foundation in light of the apostasy that surrounds them. As the *white flag of compromise* makes its way into the sky, he challenges Christians to stand with bold resolve. He writes, "But you, beloved, building yourself up in your most holy faith ..."

Recognize that the most holy faith Jude describes is the body of truth delivered by the apostles (Jude 3; Acts 2:42; Eph. 2:20) of which Christ is the cornerstone. The foundation has been sufficiently laid. *Building yourselves up (epoikodomeō)* means "to complete the structure of which the foundation has already been laid; to give yourself over to the increase of Christian knowledge and a life conformed to holiness."

Several principles flow out of Jude's encouragement. First, *commit to knowing God.* The apostle Paul sets the stage for the Christ-followers in Colossae: "And so, from the day we heard, we have not ceased to pray for you, asking that you may be filled with the knowledge of his will in all spiritual wisdom and understanding" (Col. 1:9).

To "be filled" means to be completely filled or totally controlled. Notice that Paul calls believers to be filled with *knowledge,* which implies a deep and thorough knowledge of God's will. Paul's passion is that the Colossians and all subsequent believers would integrate spiritual truth and apply biblical principles to their lives, that their lives would be an overflow of their knowledge of God. Of course, Paul's plea to the believers in Colossae was in sharp contrast to the Gnostics who were looking for some kind of "higher knowledge" to reach God. They, like the false teachers in Galatia and Jude's letter, were twisting the grace of God.

Such a commitment to being filled with a knowledge of his will leads to a worthy walk that pleases the Lord and results in an increased knowledge of God: "so as to walk in a manner worthy of the Lord, fully pleasing to him, bearing fruit in every good work and increasing in the knowledge of God" (Col. 1:10).

Second, *commit to growing in God.* Paul writes, "Therefore, as you received Christ Jesus as Lord, so walk in him, rooted and built up in him and established in the faith, just as you were taught, abounding in thanksgiving" (Col. 2:6-7). How do we move in the direction of Christian growth? Verse 6 says: "Walk in him." The Greek word which describes this "walking" is *peripateō,* and it addresses how we conduct our lives. Paul uses the same word when he writes, "*Walk* in newness of life" (Rom. 6:4) and "*Walk* by faith and not by sight" (2 Cor. 5:7). He instructs the Galatians, "*Walk* by the Spirit ..." (Gal. 5:16) and similarly challenges the Ephesian believers to "*Walk* in a manner worthy of the calling you have received" (Eph. 4:1).

We are called upon to *walk* in Christ, which comes as a result of receiving him as Lord. This way of life or *walking (peripateō)* is a present active imperative verb which suggests ongoing action committed to the Christian growth process.

Additionally, we are to be *firmly rooted* (Col. 2:7). This term is derived from the Greek word, *ridzō*, which means "to strengthen with roots; to render firm or cause something to be thoroughly grounded." Calvin takes Paul's metaphor and elaborates:

> For as a tree that has struck its roots deep has enough support for withstanding all the assaults of winds and storms, so if anyone is deeply and thoroughly fixed in Christ, as in a firm root, he cannot be thrown down from his upright position by a machination of Satan … If anyone has not fixed his roots in Christ, he will easily be carried about with every wind of doctrine, as a tree without the support of a root is blown down at the first blast.[153]

So, we not only walk in Christ, we are firmly rooted. We learn and embrace the doctrines of the faith. We immerse our minds in God's Word and develop a hunger for his truth. We water our "root systems" with God's eternal Word which not only nourishes our souls, it serves to strengthen our faith.

The apostle switches metaphors from horticulture to construction. His next plea to believers is to *get built up* (Col. 2:7). The term, *epoikodmeō* means "to finish the structure of which the foundation has already been laid and promotes an increase in Christian knowledge." In other words, the foundation of the Christian life has already been laid (Eph. 2:20). It is our responsibility to build upon this foundation and continually build our knowledge and carry out God's revealed will.

Finally, Paul the apostle challenges us to become established in the faith. He utilizes the Greek term, *bebaioō* in Colossians 2:7 which means "to make firm, establish, confirm or make sure." This crucial process ensures that we are *"becoming rooted, being built up, and established* in sound doctrine." Please understand that despite the strong movement toward "feelings" these days, that truth always pre-

---

[153] John Calvin, *Calvin's New Testament Commentaries: Vol. XI* (Grand Rapids: Eerdmans, reprint 1965), 328.

cedes experience. Placing the "experience cart" before truth leads to a lack of discernment and living according to feelings and ultimately disregards biblical imperatives.

Notice also that Paul is simply describing the *walk* of someone who has a stable faith in Christ: "For though I am absent in body, yet I am with you in spirit, rejoicing to see your good order and the firmness of your faith in Christ" (Col. 2:5). *Stereōma* or *stability* describes one who has a firm, steadfast faith which rests upon a solid foundation.

So we commit to persevering in the faith. We are firmly rooted in Christ, built up in Christ, and are established in the faith: "If you put these things before the brothers, you will be a good servant of Christ Jesus, being trained in the words of the faith and of the good doctrine that you have followed." (1 Tim. 4:6).

Depend on the Holy Spirit

The second component of the "perseverance prescription" is exclusive dependence upon the Holy Spirit. We commit to relying on his power alone. In Jude 20, the author challenges us to offer continual prayers with a God-centered orientation. Paul affirms the same reality as he encourages the Ephesian church to pray "at all times in the Spirit, with all prayer and supplication" (Eph. 6:18).

Desire God Above All

Third, Jude challenges believers, "Keep yourselves in the love of God, waiting for the mercy of our Lord Jesus Christ that leads to eternal life" (Jude 21). We must make a decisive commitment to keep ourselves in the love of God. We must bank on the facts, not question the facts. Specifically, we must guard against "love decay." Thomas Manton observes, "It is not enough to repent of gross whoredom, theft, drunkenness; we must repent also of the decays of love … Go, prosecute thyself before God for growing cold in your love and service."[154]

On October 5, 1991, I made a covenant before God and married my wife. I made a commitment to be true to my bride, to love

---

[154] Thomas Manton, *Jude* (Carlisle: Banner of Truth Trust, 1658), 347.

her until the end. The same holds true in the Christian life. When God regenerated you and you accepted Christ's free gift of salvation, you entered into a covenant. Your charge is to keep yourself in the love of God.

But Jude also reminds us to *keep watching for Christ's return.* We wait patiently for the fulfillment of Christ's promise to return for his people. The apostle Paul agrees:

> For the grace of God has appeared, bringing salvation for all people, training us to renounce ungodliness and worldly passions, and to live self-controlled, upright, and godly lives in the present age, waiting for our blessed hope, the appearing of the glory of our great God and Savior Jesus Christ (Titus 2:11–13).

> Henceforth there is laid up for me the crown of righteousness, which the Lord, the righteous judge, will award to me on that Day, and not only to me but also to all who have loved his appearing (2 Tim. 4:8).

Desiring God is a matter of perspective. When false teachers threaten to undermine your faith by hoisting the *white flag* into the sky, will you choose to focus on error or will you commit to keeping yourself in the love of God and long for his appearing? Desiring God means we choose to live out our salvation (Phil. 2:13) and we make the gospel a living reality to the watching world.

Demonstrate the Compassion of God

Finally, we are called to *demonstrate the compassion of God.* Jude challenges us to demonstrate the compassion of God to different kinds of people. Specifically, he calls us to:

- Have mercy on those who doubt (Jude 22).
- Save others by snatching them out of the fire (Jude 23).
- Show mercy with fear to false teachers (Jude 23).

The prescription for perseverance is a commitment to developing our spiritual muscles, depending on the Holy Spirit, desiring God above all, and demonstrating the compassion of Christ to his people. "Therefore, my beloved brothers, be steadfast, immovable, always abounding in the work of the Lord, knowing that in the Lord your labor is not in vain" (1 Cor. 15:58).

We have seen the importance of developing a strategic posture in this climate of compromise. Without a well thought out strategy, the church will vacillate when the prophets of postmodernity begin to pontificate. Without a time-tested strategy, the church will crumble when the winds of compromise begin to blow. Indeed, a biblical strategy must be in place to withstand the onslaught and overcome any obstacles associated with the *white flag*.

9

An Offensive Posture

"Therefore be alert, remembering that for three years I did not cease night or day to admonish every one with tears."

ACTS 20:31

As Christians, we live on the front lines. We face an ideological war, a war of ideas. Evolutionary theory reigns in the university. Pragmatism pummels the shores of the postmodern ethos. Shifting morality dominates the cultural landscape and caters to the whims of the faithless. The *white flag* continues to fly and poses a clear and present danger in the church of Jesus Christ.

We have seen the importance of maintaining a strategic posture in our generation, especially as the *white flag* grows more and more prominent. But the church has another calling, namely, we must establish an *offensive posture* in the marketplace of ideas. Paul refers to the church as a "pillar and buttress of the truth" (1 Tim. 3:15). *Hedraiōma* is the Greek term for *pillar,* a word that describes "a support." The church, then, is God's appointed means of supporting or undergirding the truth. The church is the mighty pillar that God sovereignly uses to promote and proclaim the truth.

But the truth is under attack. The truth is not only being attacked in the world, it is being assaulted within the walls of the church. Part Two examined several ways that the truth is being attacked. This assault upon the truth should come as no surprise for followers of Jesus. Scripture warns us, "For the time is coming when people will not endure sound teaching, but having itching ears they will accumulate for themselves teachers to suit their own passions, and will turn away from listening to the truth and wander off into myths" (2 Tim. 4:3–4). The reluctance to hear the truth and heed the truth will grow stronger until the return of Christ and calls for an ever-vigilant band of disciples to remain true to the gospel, even in the darkest of days.

CONTEND FOR THE FAITH

The vicious assault on the truth requires an offensive posture. So we must contend for the faith: "Beloved, although I was very eager to write to you about our common salvation, I found it necessary to write appealing to you to *contend for the faith* that was once for all delivered to the saints" (Jude 3). We must stand ready and prepare ourselves for the ongoing battle.

The Meaning of the Exhortation

The Greek term for *contend* is *èpagōnizomai*. It means "to enter a contest or compete in gymnastic games." We get a glimpse at this word at the summer and winter Olympic games. But the term has a deeper meaning than mere competition. The biblical term *contend* means to "fight with adversaries." This is strenuous activity which is carried out with great passion and zeal. Paul the apostle speaks plainly about this fight and our responsibility to maintain a strong Christian witness:

> *Fight the good fight of the faith. Take hold of the eternal life to which you were called and about which you made the good confession in the presence of many witnesses (1 Tim. 6:12).*

> *I have fought the good fight, I have finished the race, I have kept the faith (2 Tim. 4:7).*

In Jude 1:3, the author writes in the present tense; he instructs us to continually contend for the faith. We are called to fight with all our might for the truth of the gospel. Jude refers to the very essence of the Christian faith, namely, that one God eternally exists who created the world for his glory. James Orr writes, "He who with his whole heart believes in Jesus as the Son of God is thereby committed to much else besides. He is committed to a view of God, to a view of man, to a view of sin, to a view of Redemption, to a view of human destiny only found in Christianity. This forms a 'Weltanschauung' or Christian view of the world."[155]

Contending for the faith involves three critical elements. First, we must *be aware of false teachers*. In his address to the Ephesians elders, Paul says, "I know that after my departure fierce wolves will come in among you, not sparing the flock; and from among your own selves will arise men speaking twisted things, to draw away the disciples after them" (Acts 20:29–30). Being aware of false teachers involves a certain amount of knowledge. So growing in the Christian faith is a non-negotiable presupposition of every follower of Christ. Only when we know the truth will we be equipped to recognize those who peddle lies and propagate falsehood.

Second, we must *beware of false teachers*. Jesus warns, "Beware of false prophets, who come to you in sheep's clothing but inwardly are ravenous wolves" (Matt. 7:15). *Beware* (*proséchō*) is a present active imperative verb that means to be continually "on guard or alert." Jesus' warning is an urgent call to remain vigilant at all times.

Recently, there was a tragic shooting at a department store not far from where my family lives. Five people lost their lives as a gunman fired random shots among the unsuspecting. Not too many days later, I found myself wandering in the same store in a nearby city. Yet my mindset was completely different. My perspective had been transformed from a passive shopper to one whose gaze was constantly scanning the store, watching for potential danger.

Christians, too, must remain watchful and stand alert. Instead of assuming that all is well in the church, we must be on guard. Our

---

[155] James Orr, *The Christian View of God and the World* (Grand Rapids: Kregel, 1989 reprint), 4.

task is to monitor our surroundings; to pay close attention to the teaching. We must beware of false teachers.

Third, *we must share with false teachers and opponents of the faith.* Scripture says, "And the Lord's servant must not be quarrelsome but kind to everyone, able to teach, patiently enduring evil, correcting his opponents with gentleness. God may perhaps grant them repentance leading to a knowledge of the truth, and they may come to their senses and escape from the snare of the devil, after being captured by him to do his will" (2 Tim. 2:24–26). We don't merely *discern* error; we *disseminate* the truth. And we do it in such a way to win lost people. We build bridges intentionally with lost people but we never do so at the expense of truth.

Engaging in this kind of apologetic activity will require courage. Yet many Christians are simply unwilling to move in this direction: "Few are they who display the moral courage required for fidelity to God when it is unpopular or even dangerous to march to his drumbeat."[156] John MacArthur adds:

> *If not vigorously resisted, apostasy will spread like leaven through seminaries, denominations, missions agencies, and other Christian institutions. False teaching thus attacks the church like a parasite, affecting our corporate testimony, inoculating people against the real truth of the gospel, proliferating false and halfhearted 'disciples,' and filling the church with people who are actually unbelievers.* [157]

Engaging in this kind of apologetic activity implies that we stay active in the world. We refuse to withdraw from culture and become spiritual hermits. Rather, we willingly engage with lost people; we contend for the faith. Martin Luther offers a warning that should be heeded by every truth-loving follower of Christ:

> *If I profess with the loudest voice and clearest exposition every portion of the truth of God except precisely that little point which the world and the devil are at that moment attacking,*

---

[156] R.C. Sproul, *Willing to Believe: The Controversy Over Free Will* (Grand Rapids: Baker Books, 1997), 16.

[157] John F. MacArthur, *The Truth War: Fighting for Certainty in an Age of Deception*, 45.

I am not confessing Christ, however boldly I may be professing Christ. Where the battle rages there the loyalty of the soldier is proved, and to be steady on all the battlefield besides is mere flight and disgrace if he flinches at that point.[158]

COMBAT FALSE WORLDVIEWS

An offense posture involves more than merely contending for the faith. It involves engaging with the enemy. It involves combat. The Word of God describes the magnitude of the situation before us: "For certain people have crept in unnoticed who long ago were designated for this condemnation, ungodly people, who pervert the grace of our God into sensuality and deny our only Master and Lord, Jesus Christ" (Jude 4). If we are to combat false worldviews and successfully oppose the spirit of the *white flag*, we must first acknowledge the commencement of the false teachers.

The Commencement of False Teachers

Jude openly writes about a band of false teachers who wormed their way into the local church. What is even more alarming than the presence of these wolves is that no one even recognized their presence among the people of God! The church turned a blind eye to these deceivers. The *white flag* was waving and the people of God looked the other way. This practice continues in our generation. When the followers of Christ leave the back door ajar, the commencement of false teachers begins.

Paul writes about another group of false teachers, the Judaizers, who weaseled their way into the Galatian church: "Yet because of false brothers secretly brought in—who slipped in to spy out our freedom that we have in Christ Jesus, so that they might bring us into slavery" (Gal. 2:4). These godless men actively opposed what Scripture reveals, in this case, the freedom that is ours in Christ. Yet, it appears they made an unchallenged entry into the church.

Also, Peter writes about the heretics who gained a hearing among God's people: "But false prophets also arose among the people, just

---

[158] Quoted in Parker T. Williamson, *Standing Firm: Reclaiming Christian Faith in Times of Controversy* (Springfield, PA: PLC Publications, 1996), 5. See John Piper, *Contending for Our All* (Wheaton: Crossway Books, 2006), 36.

as there will be false teachers among you, who will secretly bring in destructive heresies, even denying the Master who bought them, bringing upon themselves swift destruction" (2 Pet. 2:1). Notice the influence these false teachers had on the unsuspecting: "And many will follow their sensuality, and because of them the way of truth will be blasphemed. And in their greed they will exploit you with false words" (2 Pet. 2:2-3). These gullible believers were deceived by doctrinal error, much like the wide-eyed believers in our generation who blindly follow the latest trends and teaching that appeals to the flesh.

So the wolves that Jude, Paul, and Peter identify flew in under the radar. They used deceptive means to gain a hearing among the followers of Christ. Clearly, the church failed to contend for the faith, or these false teachers never would have gained entry in the church. What should have been met with stiff opposition was granted entry into the household of faith.

The Condition of False Teachers

Jude is most likely writing about the preliminary stages of Gnosticism which would strike the church with a vengeance in a matter of years. The Gnostics taught that matter was evil and spirit was good. They taught that since the flesh was not created by God, it was proper to succumb to sinful desires. Of course, Scripture opposes this kind of worldly ideology. Such talk is not only unbiblical; it is also dangerous. Jude identifies three specific qualities in these menacing heretics. These qualities are key marks of false teachers in our generation as well:

First, *they were ungodly*. Jude utilizes the Greek term, *asebeis* to describe the condition of these false teachers. The term describes an impious person or one who is profane. This is a person who lacks a reverential awe of God. Such a person will endure the full weight of God's judgment. Peter warns, "But by the same word the heavens and earth that now exist are stored up for fire, being kept until the day of judgment and destruction of the ungodly (*asebeis*)" (2 Pet. 3:7).

Second, *they pervert the grace of God into sensuality*. The very notion of perversion suggests a massive exchange. In this case, the exchange involves trading God's grace for sensuality, a word that means "unbridled lust" or "licentiousness." The passion for promoting sensuality was not only common during Jude's day; it was also a pattern in the history of Israel. For example, in Jeremiah 2, God calls Israel to repent:

> And I brought you into a plentiful land to enjoy its fruits and its good things. But when you came in, you defiled my land and made my heritage an abomination. The priests did not say, 'Where is the Lord?' Those who handle the law did not know me; the shepherds transgressed against me; the prophets prophesied by Baal and went after things that do not profit. "Therefore I still contend with you, declares the Lord, and with your children's children I will contend. For cross to the coasts of Cyprus and see, or send to Kedar and examine with care; see if there has been such a thing" (Jer. 2:7–10).

And while Proverbs 2 warns us against pursuing a perverse path, we continue in large measure to be characterized by sensuality in our generation. Solomon says:

> Then you will understand righteousness and justice and equity, every good path; for wisdom will come into your heart, and knowledge will be pleasant to your soul; discretion will watch over you, understanding will guard you, delivering you from the way of evil, from men of perverted speech, who forsake the paths of uprightness to walk in the ways of darkness, who rejoice in doing evil and delight in the perverseness of evil, men whose paths are crooked, and who are devious in their ways (Prov. 2:9–15).

The fascination with sensuality is unprecedented in our generation. The dark path is the preferred route, while walking in the light is seen as narrow and Victorian. Sexual perversity is accepted; crude speech and degradation are the norm instead of the exception to the rule.

Third, *they deny Jesus Christ.* Jude shows the unholy progression of ungodliness which is combined with perverting the grace of God into sensuality. Such a person ultimately denies Jesus Christ. They refuse him. They reject his authority. They repudiate his sovereign lordship. They refuse to submit to his regal rule. Peter Jones shows where this kind of autonomous living leads: "Paganism is like a downward spiral. In the vortex at the bottom is Satan and the worship of evil."[159] The ultimate expression, then, of unbelief is the final denial of Jesus.

The Criteria for Detecting False Teachers

Alistair McGrath observes, "Heresy is best seen as a form of Christian belief that, more by accident than design, ultimately ends up subverting, destabilizing, or even destroying the core of the Christian faith."[160] So how do we recognize these heretics? How do we pinpoint a wolf who masquerades among the sheep? What are the warning signs of their arrival? Any combination of the denials or affirmations below is an indication that an unbiblical worldview has taken root.

False teachers deny Christ's deity. Perhaps the most famous man to deny the deity of Christ was the presbyter, Arius (ca. 256-336). The Alexandrian bishop maintained that the Son was a created being. Arius taught the Son was created by the Father. Since the Son was a creature in Arius's mind, Jesus could not possibly be eternal or immutable. But at the core of his thought was the notion that Christ was not of one substance (*homoousia*) with the Father. Instead, Arius tragically held that the Son is of a *similar substance (homoiousia)* with the Father. Anyone who follows in the footsteps of Arius is on a path to eternal judgment.

False teachers deny Christ's humanity. The Docetists taught that Jesus was divine but utterly denied the humanity of Christ. This heresy taught that Jesus only "appeared" to be human but ultimately denied the very truth of his humanity. Such of view may sound plausible but is fatally flawed.

False teachers affirm a works-based system of salvation. This appears to be the common ingredient among the dominant world religions. Paul was quick to remind the Roman believers that a works-based approach was futile:

---

[159] Peter Jones, *Gospel Truth, Pagan Lies* (Escondido: Main Entry Editions, 1999), 15.
[160] Alistair McGrath, *Heresy: A History of Defending the Truth* (New York: HarperOne, 2009), 11-12.

Now to the one who works, his wages are not counted as a gift but as his due. And to the one who does not work but believes in him who justifies the ungodly, his faith is counted as righteousness, just as David also speaks of the blessing of the one to whom God counts righteousness apart from works: "Blessed are those whose lawless deeds are forgiven, and whose sins are covered; blessed is the man against whom the Lord will not count his sin" (Rom. 4:4–8).

Isaiah adds, "We have all become like one who is unclean, and all our righteous deeds are like a polluted garment. We all fade like a leaf, and our iniquities, like the wind, take us away. There is no one who calls upon your name, who rouses himself to take hold of you; for you have hidden your face from us, and have made us melt in the hand of our iniquities" (Isa. 64:6–7). Our "works of righteousness" have no merit in the eyes of a holy God. All attempts to receive salvation by human works are futile. "For we hold that one is justified by faith apart from works of the law" (Rom. 3:28).

They affirm that salvation is unnecessary. On the other end of the spectrum is the absurd notion that we live in a self-existing universe populated by creatures which have evolved. The *American Humanist Organization*, whose motto is "Good without God" advances the idea that salvation is unnecessary. *Humanist Manifesto I* says, "Humanism believes that man is part of nature and that he has emerged as a result of a continuous process."[161] In such a scheme, salvation is not only untenable, it is considered fool-hardy at best.

The apostle John warns us, "Beloved, do not believe every spirit, but test the spirits to see whether they are from God, for many false prophets have gone out into the world" (1 John 4:1). The challenge before us is to be spiritual "truth-detectors." We must exercise biblical discernment in an age of compromise—an age which has fallen prey to the spirit of the age.

Contending for the Faith and Combatting False Worldviews

Several principles will guide our steps as we *contend* for the faith and *combat* false worldviews:

---

[161] https://americanhumanist.org/what-is-humanism/manifesto1/

1. Cultivate a basic understanding of the dominant worldviews. This will take time and will require sacrifice. We must be courageous as we sort through the dubious philosophical and theological speculation of the day. Churches must offer basic training that establishes believers and trains them to understand the various worldviews of our age.

2. Create a safeguard in our hearts and minds against false worldviews. Scripture admonishes us to stand our ground and be alert: "See to it that no one takes you captive by philosophy and empty deceit, according to human tradition, according to the elemental spirits of the world, and not according to Christ" (Col. 2:8). This imperative must be rigidly adhered to. There is no room for compromise in this evil generation.

3. Cling to the truth. Wise is the Christian who heeds the warnings of Francis Schaeffer that we observed in the introduction. We not only adhere to the truth, we make a bold and decisive declaration: "*We will never compromise the truth!*" Os Guinness, who wrote twenty-five years after Schaeffer's original admonition, summarizes the four main components of compromise. These incremental steps begin small, as Guinness observes. But small steps of compromise eventually lead to massive worldview shifts and doctrinal deviations. These seismic shifts fundamentally alter how we think and how we behave. Note the four components of compromise that Guinness sets forth:[162]

- *Assumption:* The road to compromise begins with small steps. We may give credence to or acknowledge an ideology that conflicts with the Christian worldview. In essence, we open the door to the possibility of a lie being true.
- *Abandonment:* Everything that does not fit within the new assumption is discarded.
- *Adaption:* Something new is assumed, something old is abandoned, and everything else is adapted. Thus, we find various denominations adapting what they believe.
- *Assimilation:* Christian assumptions are absorbed by erroneous views. The gospel becomes assimilated to fit the

---

[162] Os Guinness, *Dining with the Devil* (Grand Rapids: Baker Book House, 1993), 56-57.

shape of the culture. The small incremental steps that were achieved during adaption lead to assimilation, which is a pathway to apostasy.

4. Commit to the Christian worldview. Finally, an offensive posture requires that we make a steadfast effort to developing our minds for God's glory. D.A. Carson urges, "… The good news of Jesus Christ is virtually incoherent unless it is securely set into a biblical worldview."[163] Making such a commitment will require time and discipline. It will require careful study and prayer. To do any less invites the horrendous effects of compromise to invade our lives and cripple our churches.

After the terrorist attack on 9/11, the Bush administration conducted an investigation to determine if Saddam Hussein possessed weapons of mass destruction. Even though coalition troops failed to unearth these weapons, the debate continues: Did Saddam destroy any weapons of mass destruction prior to the invasion of Iraq? Or did the Bush administration jump to an unwarranted conclusion? Perhaps we will never know.

One thing is certain: *Weapons of mass destruction* are a daily reality for followers of Jesus Christ. These weapons are in the realm of ideas. Scripture acknowledges these ideas which constantly wage war against the Christian worldview: "For we do not wrestle against flesh and blood, but against the rulers, against the authorities, against the cosmic powers over this present darkness, against the spiritual forces of evil in the heavenly places" (Eph. 6:12).

The Word of God calls us to utterly demolish ideas that are contrary to Scripture: "We destroy arguments and every lofty opinion raised against the knowledge of God, and take every thought captive to obey Christ" (2 Cor. 10:5). The consequences of following the crowd and capitulating to the ideas of the world are grim, indeed (Ps. 1:4-6). Dean Inge remarks, "He who marries the spirit of the age will soon become a widower."[164]

---

[163] D.A. Carson, *The Gagging of God* (Grand Rapids: Zondervan Publishing House, 1996), 502.

[164] Dean Inge as cited in Os Guinness, *Dining with the Devil*, 63.

So, we must maintain an offensive posture. We must *contend* for the faith and *combat* faithlessness in our pluralistic culture. Let us rise together and stand against every strand of apostasy and engage in worldview warfare to the glory of God.

10

A Vigilant Posture

"I glory in the distinguishing grace of God, and will not, by the grace of God, step one inch from my principles, or think of adhering to the present fashionable sort of religion."

C.H. SPURGEON

The historic Christian faith is grounded and rooted in the truth. Scripture reminds us that the church is "a pillar and buttress of truth" (1 Tim. 3:15). We might compare the truth to a shrub or a flower in a potted plant. Whenever my wife gets a new plant, she sends me to the store to purchase a bag of potting soil. She then puts on a pair of gloves, pours the soil in the pot, and proceeds to carefully plant the flowers. Next, she mixes in some *Miracle Grow* for good measure. She strategically places the flowers where they will receive the right amount of sunshine. Finally, she makes a commitment to watering her flowers, not only initially, but on a daily basis.

Likewise, in this age of compromise, we as Christ-followers need to be careful with the truth. We must *tend* the truth. In this day in which the *white flag* flies proudly in the marketplace of ideas, we must commit ourselves to nurturing the truth. We must determine to always be attentive to the truth. We must maintain a vigilant posture.

One of the distinguishing qualities of a growing Christian, then, is an ever-increasing knowledge of the truth:

> *And it is my prayer that your love may abound more and more, with knowledge and discernment ... (Phil. 1:9).*

> *... That you may be filled with the knowledge of his will in all spiritual wisdom and understanding, so as to walk in a manner worthy of the Lord, fully pleasing to him, bearing fruit in every good work and increasing in the knowledge of God (Col. 1:9-10).*

While the Bible continually calls upon the people of God to grow in the knowledge of the truth, a troubling trend plagues the church. At its root is a growing antipathy directed at the intellect. Francis Schaeffer detected this deadly virus over fifty years ago. The virus in our day has grown even more pronounced and continues to ravage the church: "This has been one of the weaknesses of evangelical, orthodox Christianity - we have been proud in despising philosophy, and we have been exceedingly proud in despising the intellect."[165] We must repudiate this escalating trend that militates against the Christian mind.

The apostle Paul explains that the heart of the elect is characterized by a faith which is *grounded*, a knowledge of the truth which is *growing*, and godliness which is *showing*. He explains that the hope of the elect is eternal life with the living God. His passion for the truth is plain in Titus 1:1-4:

> *Paul, a servant of God and an apostle of Jesus Christ, for the sake of the faith of God's elect and their knowledge of the truth, which accords with godliness, in hope of eternal life, which God, who never lies, promised before the ages began and at the proper time manifested in his word through the preaching with which I have been entrusted by the command of God our Savior; To Titus, my true child in a common faith: Grace and peace from God the Father and Christ Jesus our Savior.*

---

[165] Francis A. Schaeffer, *The Complete Works of Francis A. Schaeffer: He Is There and He Is Not Silent* (Wheaton: Crossway Books, 1982), 279.

After Paul's greeting to Titus, he instructs him to "appoint elders" in the church (Titus 1:5). He proceeds to unpack the qualifications for the office of elder. The final qualification in Paul's list has special significance for our study as it concerns the matter of truth: "He must hold firm to the trustworthy word as taught, so that he may be able to give instruction in sound doctrine and also to rebuke those who contradict it" (Titus 1:9).

We have witnessed the *white flag* which has been proudly displayed outside the perimeter of the church. The sad reality is that many people in postmodern culture pay no regard to the truth. They will do anything they can to stifle the truth, minimize the truth, and even outright reject the truth. We have also seen some within the church who tolerate the *white flag* or even rejoice in the blatant compromise it represents.

Our task as followers of Christ, then, is to maintain a vigilant posture. This posture requires that we understand the problem, formulate a plan, and set forth a purpose.

THE PROBLEM

One of the major reasons that elders are called upon to be champions of the truth is that some people are undermining the truth. But elders are not the only ones who have a responsibility to stand boldly for the truth. All Christ-followers must embrace the truth and defend the truth.

People Are Undermining the Truth

Instead of loving the truth, heeding the truth, and nurturing the truth, people are quick to undermine the truth. They won't think twice about uprooting the truth and casting it into the nearest trash pail.

The Scriptures teach that many people actively oppose the truth (Titus 1:10). This was no isolated issue in the first-century church. It certainly is not an isolated issue in the church today. Some of the people who undermine the truth do so in the church (Jude 3-4; 2 Pet. 2:1-3). Titus 1:10-16 provides several vivid examples of what this opposition looks like:

For there are many who are insubordinate, empty talkers and deceivers, especially those of the circumcision party. They must be silenced, since they are upsetting whole families by teaching for shameful gain what they ought not to teach. One of the Cretans, a prophet of their own, said, "Cretans are always liars, evil beasts, lazy gluttons." This testimony is true. Therefore rebuke them sharply, that they may be sound in the faith, not devoting themselves to Jewish myths and the commands of people who turn away from the truth. To the pure, all things are pure, but to the defiled and unbelieving, nothing is pure; but both their minds and their consciences are defiled. They profess to know God, but they deny him by their works. They are detestable, disobedient, unfit for any good work.

People who undermine the truth may be guilty of any number of these sinful qualities. Each quality undermines the truth. The opponents of the truth come in different shades and colors. Some people are on a mission to destroy the church. This active rebellion is prompted by malice and driven by heretical musings. Other people may not be actively seeking to do harm to the church, but somewhere along the way, they become ensnared by sin. Their hearts grow hard and become bitter. Unresolved sin leads to broken relationships which give the devil a foothold. Sometimes this sin may be traced back many years ago. Sin which is never fully repented of grows like a cancer and begins to poison the church.

Before we look at the problem that Titus faced, take some time to consider a serious question: *Is it possible that you have become ensnared by sin? Is it possible that unconfessed sin is paying negative dividends in your family, at your place of employment, or in your church?* Will you echo the prayer of David? "Search me, O God, and know my heart! Try me and know my thoughts! And see if there be any grievous way in me, and lead me in the way everlasting!" (Ps. 139:23–24). Are you willing to do business with God? Ask the Holy Spirit to surface any sin in your life. Deal with it now. Take it to the cross and find freedom and forgiveness!

Paul lists some specific marks of a person who undermines the truth in Titus 1:10-16.

Insubordinate (v. 10)

The Greek word, *anupótaktos* describes a person who is rebellious; a person who will not submit to authority; a person who stands in defiance of the authority that God has placed in his or her life.[166]

Insubordination is one of the most damaging things a local church must face. While insubordination may appear cavalier to some, it is a reckless evil that will divide a church and subtly contribute to the progress of the *white flag*.

Insubordinate people are quick to make excuses and hurl insults on others - anything to avoid the horrific implications of being held accountable for this God-dishonoring sin.

Empty talkers (v. 10)

An empty talker (*mataiológos*) is "an idle talker; someone whose talk is worthless drivel." Such a person is a legalistic hairsplitter. Empty talkers are windbags with the potential to split a church. Warren Wiersbe adds, "They were vain talkers. What they said impressed people, but it had no content or substance. When you 'boiled it down,' it was just so much hot air. Furthermore, they excelled in talking, not in doing. They could tell others what to do, but they did not do it themselves."[167] Empty talkers have much to say and very little to contribute until they learn to submit to the lordship of Christ in their lives.

Deceivers (v. 10)

A deceiver (*phrenapáteis*) is a person who leads others astray. This person is an expert at convincing others to believe things which are not true. Ever since the original lie in the Garden of Eden, deceivers have been "pulling the wool" over the eyes of the sheep and will continue to make progress until elders and truth-loving Christians address their evil ruse.

---

[166] The same word occurs in 1 Tim. 1:9 and is translated as "disobedient." The word is used in the same breath as those who are lawless, ungodly, unholy, and profane.

[167] Wiersbe, W. W. (1996). The Bible exposition commentary (Vol. 2, p. 262). Wheaton, IL: Victor Books.

People who promote works-based salvation (v. 10)

Paul refers to these as the "circumcision party," those who reject the doctrines of grace and rely on good works. In Galatians 2:4 he addressed the *pseudadelphos,* or "false brothers." He identifies their mission, which was to "spy out our freedom that we have in Christ." The purpose is "so that they might bring us into slavery."

It is doubtful that we will come face-to-face with a card-carrying member of the "circumcision party" in our day. But the propensity to promote works-based salvation is still alive and well. Any addition to grace is a false gospel. John Stott says, "The Christian has been set free from the law in the sense that his acceptance before God depends entirely upon God's grace in the death of Jesus Christ received by faith. To introduce the works of the law and make our acceptance depend on our obedience to rules and regulations was to bring a free man into bondage again."[168]

Teaching for shameful gain (v. 11)

Paul says these shameful teachers were "upsetting whole families" with their well-crafted heresies. The Greek term *ánatrépō* is translated as "upsetting." The term means "to ruin or overturn one's faith." The same word is used in 2 Timothy 2:17-18 when Paul warned Timothy to avoid the false teachers Hymenaeus and Philetus, who "swerved from the truth." These doctrinal deviators were "upsetting the faith of some." This became such a problem in the first-century church that Paul said, "They must be silenced."

Liars, evil beasts, and lazy gluttons (vv. 12-13)

Paul cites Epimenedes, a Cretan philosopher/poet, a man who was considered to be a prophet who said, "Cretans are always liars, evil beasts, lazy gluttons. This testimony is true" (Titus 1:12-13). Cretans were stereotyped as liars because they claimed the tomb of Zeus was located on Crete.[169] These people were committed to the pursuit of sinful pleasure. Such people were also identified by Paul in 2 Tim-

---

[168] John R.W. Stott, *The Message of Galatians* (Downers Grove: InterVarsity Press, 1968), 43.

[169] Larson, K. (2000). *I & II Thessalonians, I & II Timothy, Titus,* Philemon (Vol. 9, p. 346). Nashville, TN: Broadman & Holman Publishers.

othy 3:4, as "treacherous, reckless, swollen with conceit, lovers of pleasure rather than lovers of God."

Turning away from the truth (v. 14)

It should come as no surprise that people who undermine the truth also turn away from the truth. The Greek word *àpostréphō* is translated as "turn away." It means "to cause a person to change their belief structure; to forsake the truth." This problem has only grown worse in the current milieu. In our generation, it is fashionable to turn away from the truth. However, Jesus issues a stern warning to anyone who turns a person away from the truth:

> *Whoever receives one such child in my name receives me, but whoever causes one of these little ones who believe in me to sin, it would be better for him to have a great millstone fastened around his neck and to be drowned in the depth of the sea. "Woe to the world for temptations to sin! For it is necessary that temptations come, but woe to the one by whom the temptation comes!" (Matt. 18:5–7).*

Defiled minds and consciences (vv. 15-16)

People who undermine the truth have *defiled minds* and *defiled consciences*. They make a profession of faith but deny God by their works. In 2 Timothy 3:5, Paul says these people have the "appearance of godliness" but deny its power. The Greek word, translated *deny,* means "to refuse to agree; to disagree; to refuse to follow."

Jesus' warning for such a person is vivid: "but whoever denies me before men, I also will deny before my Father who is in heaven" (Matt. 10:33). The apostle John goes further by saying that a truth denier is in league with the antichrist: "Who is the liar but he who denies that Jesus is the Christ? This is the antichrist, he who denies the Father and the Son. No one who denies the Son has the Father. Whoever confesses the Son has the Father also" (1 John 2:22–23).

Paul concludes his brutal portrait of the one who undermines the truth by noting that they are "detestable, disobedient, unfit for any good work." Scripture offers a plain warning for anyone who undermines the truth. The problems that plagued the church in the first-century continue to infest the church today. The portrait of the troubled church in our day is nothing to trifle with.

THE PORTRAIT OF A TROUBLED CHURCH

We live in a sinful world, polluted by the fall of man and poisoned by depraved minds. The church is not immune from such depravity. We not only find carnality running rampant in the world, we find that the hideous effects of sin plague the church as well.

America is filled with churches in which carnality reigns and sin goes unchecked. Whenever we allow sin to go unrestrained, it will spread like a virus from person to person. In such a setting, sin is minimized. Sin is ignored. Sin may even be celebrated. Leadership turns a deaf ear to the very thing that threatens to tear apart the fabric of what was once cherished. Some churches resist church discipline. They promise to "love" at all costs. These churches attract people in droves. But the result is a weakened church in which holiness becomes a distant memory and carnality becomes the new "normal."

This kind of compromise is crippling the church. It is a problem that cannot go unaddressed. In Titus 1:9, the apostle Paul says that a qualified elder must have a commitment to the truth by rebuking opponents of the truth. He gives Titus instructions on how to deal with the people who are sabotaging the truth. These instructions set forth a specific plan for confronting the compromise which is crippling the local church.

THE PLAN

Paul instructs Titus to respond in two decisive ways when a person opposes or undermines the truth. Both of these action steps are written in the present tense, which indicates an activity that never ceases. When an opponent of the truth surfaces, elders must respond swiftly and obediently. Elders are not the only ones who engage in this activity. Whenever we as followers of Jesus face doctrinal error or compromise, we must respond in like manner.

Extinguish the Opponents of the Truth

First, *we must extinguish opponents of the truth*. Titus 1:11 says, "They must be silenced." The Greek term for silence, *épistomizō*, means "to change an opinion; to muzzle; to stop the mouth." This term runs contrary to the typical pluralistic drivel that controls our universities and even some churches. But Paul is clear here. Those who undermine the truth - the insubordinate, empty talkers, and deceivers - must be silenced.

When a fire breaks out, the firemen come and extinguish the flames. If the fire is not smothered, the structure will soon be destroyed. In the same way, when people who undermine the truth in the church are not silenced, the church eventually ends up in a pile of ashes. In the case of many European churches, the ornate buildings may remain but the people who make their way down the aisle are merely participating in a tour. The churches that once proclaimed the glory of God's grace have been transformed into money-making museums.

Expose the Enemies of the Truth

Second, *we must expose the enemies of the truth*. Paul says, "This testimony is true. Therefore rebuke them sharply, that they may be sound in the faith, not devoting themselves to Jewish myths and the commands of people who turn away from the truth" (Titus 1:13-14). *Rebuke them sharply* comes from the Greek term, *élegchō* which means "to cut with an axe or knife with penetrating force." Rebuking an enemy of the truth involves calling attention to their fault. This important activity exposes the sinfulness of sin and unbelief!

Jesus underscores the importance of exposing wickedness: "For everyone who does wicked things hates the light and does not come to the light, lest his works should be exposed" (*élegchō*). Paul adds, "Take no part in the unfruitful works of darkness, but instead *expose* (*élegchō*) them" (Eph. 5:11). He continues, "But when anything is *exposed* (*élegchō*) by the light, it becomes visible" (Eph. 5:13).

The charge to rebuke an enemy of the truth suggests something that is cast aside by most people in contemporary culture. The charge to rebuke an enemy of the truth suggests a right and a wrong. Certainly, such a proposal is an unsavory prospect but this crucial activity is a normal part of living the Christian life. For instance, an expositional preaching ministry involves *rebuking* those who are in error (2 Tim. 4:2). Elders are charged with *rebuking* anyone who contradicts sound doctrine (Titus 1:9). Christ-followers are charged with *rebuking* a brother or sister who sins against them (Matt. 18:15).

One of the most well-known rebukes takes place when Nathan rebukes David for the sin of adultery (2 Sam. 12:1-15). After presenting David with a story that involved a man who was treated unjustly, Nathan confronts the man ensnared in sin. "You are the man!" says Nathan (v. 7).

Sin must be exposed and confessed and repented of in order for Christ-followers to lives healthy lives before God. Likewise, sin must be exposed and confessed and repented of in the local church if she is to have any influence on a watching pagan culture. The Bible clearly describes the importance of biblical confrontation: "Whoever loves discipline loves knowledge, but he who hates reproof is stupid" (Prov. 12:1). Proverbs 15:10 says, "There is severe discipline for him who forsakes the way; whoever hates reproof will die." And Proverbs 10:17b warns, "…But he who rejects reproof leads others astray."

The Bible demands a two-fold plan for confronting people who undermine the truth. Yet, how many times do we ignore people who undermine the truth? How many times do we side-step people who undermine the truth? How many times do we justify people who willingly undermine the truth claims of God's Word? Now is the time for a decisive plan that upholds the truth of God's revealed truth.

THE PURPOSE

Finally, Titus 1:13 reveals a critical purpose for exposing the opponents of the truth. "Therefore rebuke them sharply, that they may be sound in the faith."

Divine Shelter

Every person who undermines the truth lives in direct opposition to God's revelation. A stern rebuke, therefore, actually serves those who repudiate the truth. Exposing and confronting sin provides a shelter which will ensure a framework for healthy Christian living. The Greek word translated *sound (úgiainō) means "to be healthy; accurate; pure; sound in the faith."* The *New Living Translation* (NLT) translates the word as *"strong in the faith."* The ministry of rebuke is meant to have positive and life-changing effects! Notice how the writer of Proverbs describes the outcome of such a ministry:

> *The ear that listens to the life-giving reproof will dwell among the wise (Prov. 15:31).*

> *Poverty and disgrace come to him who ignores instruction, but whoever heeds reproof is honored (Prov. 13:18).*

> *Whoever heeds instruction is on the path to life ... (Prov. 10:17a).*

Providing this kind of shelter helps guard the doctrinal integrity of the local church *and* protects the flock from deceivers and people who have turned from the truth. This shelter helps protect the unity of the church, especially since false teachers are experts at sowing seeds of division and "upsetting families" (Titus 1:11). This shelter helps protect the biblical authority structure in a local church. This shelter helps new believers and the unsuspecting.

Galatians 5:19-20 says, "Now the works of the flesh are evident: sexual immorality, impurity, sensuality, idolatry, sorcery, enmity, strife, jealousy, fits of anger, rivalries, dissensions, divisions." The Greek term *aíresis*, translated as *divisions* in this passage is also the same term for *heresy*. Heresy involves more than merely believing and spreading false doctrine. Heresy involves the sin of division and divisiveness. The sin of division is included among the things that the LORD hates. Proverbs 6:19 reveals a God who hates "a false witness who breathes out lies, and one who sows discord among brothers."

The Bible demands nothing less than unity in the body of Christ: "I therefore, a prisoner for the Lord, urge you to walk in a manner worthy of the calling to which you have been called, with all humility and gentleness, with patience, bearing with one another in love, eager to maintain the unity of the Spirit in the bond of peace" (Eph. 4:1–3). God places a premium on unity, so much that it is at the very center of God's purposes for the church. Unity is something that is attained. The aim of unity, according to Ephesians 4:13, is "mature manhood, to the measure of the stature of the fulness of Christ."

Peter highlights this unity in 1 Peter 3:8. He writes, "Finally, all of you, have unity (ómophrōn) of mind, sympathy, brotherly love, a tender heart, and a humble mind." This is the unity that should prevail in the local church. This kind of unity is contagious.

The challenge before us is to be united around the truth or become mired in divisiveness. We find an incredible example of unity in the Old Testament. In Nehemiah 8:1-6, the people ask Ezra to "bring the book." They are unified around their desire to sit under the teaching ministry of God's Word. These people were attentive to the Word of God. They were unified in their desire to listen and pay attention to Scripture: "And he read from it facing the square before the Water Gate from early morning until midday, in the presence of the men and the women and those who could understand. And the ears of all the people were attentive to the Book of the Law" (Neh.8:3).

The people also responded reverently to God's Word. They were unified in their posture before the authority of God: "And Ezra blessed the Lord, the great God, and all the people answered, 'Amen, Amen,' lifting up their hands. And they bowed their heads and worshiped the Lord with their faces to the ground" (Neh. 8:6).

Finally, the people responded in worship as they were confronted with the truth of God's Word. They were unified in their adoration and worship. Look carefully at their response: "And all the people went their way to eat and drink and to send portions and to make great rejoicing, because they had understood the words that were declared to them" (Neh. 8:12). They were fixated on one thing. They bowed in complete submission to the sovereign God of the universe!

Have you become ensnared by the sin of division? Is it possible that you have given the devil a foothold? Have you subtly sown seeds of discord in your church?

CONCLUSION

We have examined the challenged church and faced some of the most daunting obstacles in our path. We have seen the destructive nature of compromise in the church. We have witnessed the horrifying effects of a dismantled God, a disregarded doctrine, and a denigrated work of Christ. We have seen how the judgment of Christ has been discarded and we bear witness to the demolition of the Christian mind.

But we have also extended a call to the church. This call involves a posture which is strategic, defensive, and vigilant. This call extends to Christ-followers in churches from the village to the city. Heeding this call is essential if we have any hope of reaching the next generation for Christ.

Francis Schaeffer spent his life warning the church about the dangers of compromise:

> *Woe, O liberal church! Woe, O apostate Christendom! Spiritual adultery, mind you, against the only adequate Bridegroom for man—sindividual man and mankind - the only adequate Bridegroom for all people in all the world. Spiritual adultery against the only One who can fulfill the longing of the human heart. To turn away from the divine Bridegroom is to turn to unfulfillment. This is not only sin; it is destruction.*[170]

The call to the church is not ambiguous. The die has been cast. The lines have been drawn. Our marching orders are clearly set forth in the Word of God. We must stand strong in these days of compromise. We must withstand the assaults of the evil one. We must resist the *white flag* of compromise in the strength God provides.

The *white flag* will continue to fly until Jesus returns. On that glorious day, he will vanquish his enemies and vindicate his people. However, until his triumphant return, we must live and proclaim the great realities of the gospel, holding high the banner of truth. To do any less is to capitulate to the whims of the world and surrender to the strategy of the enemy.

---

[170] Francis A. Schaeffer, *The Church Before the Watching World* (Wheaton: Crossway Books, reprint 1982), 147.

EPILOGUE

We Pledge Allegiance

⊷⋯⋯⋯◆⋯⋯⋯⊶

istory is a fine teacher that reminds us of the past and
helps chart the path into the future. The lessons of the
Second World War remind us that unchecked evil will
immobilize men and paralyze nations. Fascism and com-
munism were the evil twin menaces that sought to bring the free world
to its knees in the twentieth century. The likes of Winston Churchill,
Alexander Solzhenitsyn, Franklin Delano Roosevelt, and Ronald Rea-
gan stood with steadfast resolve against the enemies of freedom.

The enemy of freedom birthed during the Second World War
was an atheistic contagion that recoiled at the very notion of God.
In our generation, a new breed of terror has hatched and threatens to
devour freedom as we know it. While many are rightly concerned by
the rise of global terrorism, followers of Jesus Christ should be even
more alarmed by the theological terrorism which has infiltrated the
church.

Francis Schaeffer warned us about the "drift" that was taking
place in the church. Therefore, we must stand prepared, ready to
contend with the *white flag* of compromise. We must recognize the
existential threat that exists in the church. We must respond with the
courage of Daniel and the steely resolve of Gideon. We must prepare
our minds for action (1 Pet. 1:13) and wield the mighty sword of the
Spirit (Eph. 6:17). We must not only refuse to waver, we must stand
with steadfastness in the face of compromise.

C.H. Spurgeon stood with bold resolve in nineteenth century London, even in the midst of theological capitulation. His call to the faithful, then, serves as both a warning and an encouragement to battle-weary soldiers: "O brethren, (he said to his pastors' conference) we shall soon have to die! We look each other in the face today in health, but there will come a day when others will look down upon our pallid countenances as we lie in our coffins ... It will matter little to us who shall gaze upon us then, but it will matter eternally how we have discharged our work during our lifetime."[171]

Surely, the Prince of Preachers would have heartily approved of this anonymous charge:

> *Stick with your work. Do not flinch because of the lions' roars; Do not stop to stone the devil's dogs; Do not fool away your time chasing the devil's rabbits. Do your work. Let liars lie, let sectarians quarrel, let critics malign, let enemies accuse, let the devil do his worst; But see to it nothing hinders you from fulfilling with joy the work God has given you. He has not commanded you to be admired or esteemed. He has never bidden you to defend your character. He has not set you at work to contradict falsehood which Satan's or God's servants may start to peddle, or to track down every rumor that threatened your reputation. If you do these things, you will do nothing else; you will be at work for yourself and not for the Lord. Keep at your work. Let your aim be steady as a star. You may be assaulted, wronged, insulted, slandered, wounded and rejected, misunderstood, or assigned impure motives; You may be abused by foes, forsaken by friends, and despised and rejected by men. But see to it with steadfast determination with unfaltering zeal, that you pursue the great purpose of your life and object of your being until at last you can say, "I have finished the work which Thou gavest me to do."*

The *white flag* flies proudly above the church and invites the ill-informed and the weak-kneed to join her ranks. Who will stand in this age of compromise? Who will march with bold resolve and carry the torch of truth? Who will faithfully serve in the face of such compromise?

---

[171] C.H. Spurgeon, *An All Round Ministry*, 76.

The *white flag* will continue to soar and the masses will stand in allegiance before her godless anthem. Most people will tolerate compromise and many will welcome it wholeheartedly. Yet God calls his people to a different standard, one that is high and holy. We are called to live according to the gospel. We are called to be a people of conviction. So we pledge allegiance to our sovereign Savior who orchestrates all things for his glory. We refuse to allow compromise to cripple the church. We pay homage to Jesus Christ and bow to no other.

Soli Deo Gloria!

APPENDIX 1

If the Foundations Are Destroyed

E very nation has an assortment of pivotal events that mark a series of decisive turning points which influence culture, politics, worldviews, and religious views. Some of these turning points include things like the assassinations of Abraham Lincoln or John Fitzgerald Kennedy. Other pivotal events have occurred in the political area such as the Vietnam War or Watergate. Of course, 9/11 was a critical turning point in the life of our nation.

A turning point may take place with the swing of a gavel. One such turning point took place in 1973 as the Supreme Court legalized abortion on demand. The most recent turning point occurred on June 29, 2015. On that day, we woke up in a different nation. In a historic move, the Supreme Court rendered a decision by a vote of 5-4, which rendered same-sex marriage a legal right for all Americans.

Christians from Seattle to Orlando and Los Angeles to New York City worked through a whole range of emotions, including disappointment, grief, anger, frustration, and apprehension about the future. Our challenge is to face a series of crucial questions: "What does this mean for me?" "What does this mean for my church?" "What does this mean for my country?"

The dilemma we face as a nation, which comes as a result of the Supreme Court decision is nothing new. The people of God have faced such seasons of adversity and compromise throughout redemptive history:

- *God's people were oppressed by Pharaoh and forced to work as slaves* (Exod. 1:13).
- *God's people lived among idol worshipers who do what is right in their own eyes* (Judges 21:25).
- *God's people lived under the thumb of Nebuchadnezzar who mandated the worship of an image made of gold* (Dan. 3:1).
- *God's people were taken into captivity by rival nations who were cruel and ruthless* (Hab. 1:6).
- *In New Testament days, God's people lived in the shadow of evil men like Herod.*
- *Christians endured the evil reign of men like Joseph Stalin in the former Soviet Union and Adolf Hitler in Germany.*

Events in the early church taught Christ-followers to live under intense persecution. They were oppressed by tyrants like Nero and Diocletian. Bruce Shelly describes the 1st-century believer as one who is fundamentally different:

> *Men always view with suspicion people who are different. Conformity, not distinctiveness, is the way to a trouble-free life. So the more early Christians took their faith seriously the more they were in danger of crowd reaction … Thus, simply by living according to the teachings of Jesus, the Christian was a constant outspoken condemnation of the pagan way of life. It was not that the Christian went about criticizing and condemning and disapproving, nor was he consciously self-righteous and superior. It was simply that Christian ethic in itself was a criticism of pagan life.*[172]

In the third-century, Emperor Decius (249-251) made Caesar worship mandatory for every race and nation with the single exception of the Jews:

---

[172] Bruce Shelly, *Church History in Plain Language* (Nashville: Thomas Nelson, 1995), 39.

On a certain day in the year, every Roman citizen had to come to the Temple of Caesar and had to burn a pinch of incense there and say: 'Caesar is Lord.' When he had done that, he was given a certificate to guarantee that he had done so. After a man had burned his pinch of incense and had acknowledged Caesar as Lord, he could go away and worship any god he liked, so long as the worship did not affect public decency and order.[173]

Shelly explains:

If a man refused to carry out the ceremony of acknowledging Caesar, he was automatically branded as a traitor and a revolutionary ... Thus, Christian worship and Caesar worship met head-on. The one thing that no Christian would ever say: 'Caesar is Lord.' For the Christian, Jesus Christ and he alone was Lord ... Had the Christians been willing to burn that pinch of incense and to say formally, 'Caesar is Lord,' they could have gone on worshiping Christ to their heart's content; but the Christians would not compromise. That is why Rome regarded them as a band of potential revolutionaries threatening the very existence of the empire.[174]

Move forward 1,300 years as Mary Tudor (1555-1558) had nearly 300 Protestants burned at the stake for their faith and devotion to the Lord Jesus Christ. Her cruel reign struck fear in the hearts of the godly.

This short survey only scratches the surface. Suffice it to say, suffering is certainly not a new experience for followers of Christ. Living under the tyrannical thumb of a dictator or under the dictates of a judge is something that Christians have experienced throughout church history.

The question is posed: *In light of the Supreme Court's decision to legalize same-sex marriage, how shall we as Christ-followers respond?* The question is set forth in a more general way in Psalm 11:3, "If the foundations are destroyed, what can the righteous do?"

---

[173] Ibid.
[174] Ibid.

As Christians, it is crucial that we approach the Supreme Court decision with a humble attitude and a God-centered perspective. The Word of God alone must shape our mindset and mold our interactions with people, believers and unbelievers alike. In short, our approach must be informed and driven by the gospel. How, then, shall we as Christ-followers respond? Will we stand by passively as the *white flag* makes its ascent into the postmodern stratosphere? Or will we respond with stalwart biblical conviction and obedience? I urge followers of Christ to give serious consideration to three responses.

THREE RESPONSES

Make a Crucial Commitment: We uphold the biblical portrait of marriage.

There are at least five reasons to believe that Scripture establishes God's design for marriage between one man and one woman. Kevin DeYoung observes:

1. The way in which the woman was created indicates that she is the man's divinely designed complement (Gen. 2:21-22).

2. The nature of the one-flesh union presupposes two persons of the opposite sex (Gen. 2:25).

3. Only two persons of the opposite sex can fulfill the procreative purposes of marriage.

4. Jesus himself reinforces the Genesis account (Matt. 19:4-6).

5. The cover-to-cover significance of marriage as a divine symbol in the Bible only works if the marital couple is a complementary pair.[175]

No court has the authority to redefine what God has established in his Word. Therefore, let us commit ourselves to the biblical portrait of marriage. May we make this bold resolution: *We will never compromise the truth!*

---

[175] Kevin DeYoung, *What Does the Bible Really Teach About Homosexuality?* (Wheaton: Crossway Books, 2015), Kindle edition, Loc. 238-308.

Model the Gospel: We resolve to enter the marketplace with truth and grace.

We model the gospel by paying due respect to the Supreme Court. God's Word is clear on this matter:

> *Let every person be subject to the governing authorities. For there is no authority except from God, and those that exist have been instituted by God. Therefore whoever resists the authorities resists what God has appointed, and those who resist will incur judgment (Rom. 13:1–2).*

> *Be subject for the Lord's sake to every human institution, whether it be to the emperor as supreme, or to governors as sent by him to punish those who do evil and to praise those who do good (1 Pet. 2:13–14).*

We model the gospel by disobeying any decision or legislation that is in conflict with God's Word. In the Old Testament, King Nebuchadnezzar commanded Shadrach, Meshach, and Abednego to bow down and worship the golden statue (Dan. 3:11). Pay close attention to the response of these godly men: "But if not, be it known to you, O king, that we will not serve your gods or worship the golden image that you have set up" (Dan. 3:18).

In the early days of the church, the Sanhedrin commanded the apostles to stop preaching the gospel (Acts 4:18). Notice the response of the apostles: "But Peter and John answered them, "Whether it is right in the sight of God to listen to you rather than to God, you must judge, for we cannot but speak of what we have seen and heard" (Acts 4:19-20). In Acts 5:29, Peter and the apostles respond with boldness and courage: "We must obey God rather than men."

We model the gospel by reaching out to the homosexual community. We care for homosexual sinners in the same way we care for heterosexual sinners (1 Cor. 6:9-11). Please remember that every person, homosexual and heterosexual alike is an image-bearer of God, created with worth, value, and dignity. We are called to:

- Love our neighbors regardless of whatever disagreements arise as a result of conflicting beliefs about marriage;

- Live respectfully and civilly alongside those who may disagree with us for the sake of the common good;
- Cultivate a common culture of religious liberty that allows the freedom to live and believe differently to prosper.[176]

We call homosexuals to repentance in the same way we call heterosexual sinners to repentance. No doubt, both heterosexuals and homosexuals will reject our call to repentance; others, however, will marvel at the Savior and be saved (Acts 16:31; 17:30-31). Indeed, every sexual sinner must repent and turn his or her attention to the cross of the Lord Jesus Christ!

We model the gospel when we respond in a godly fashion when persecution strikes. Paul reminds us, "Indeed, all who desire to live a godly life in Christ Jesus will be persecuted, while evil people and imposters will go on from bad to worse, deceiving and being deceived" (2 Tim. 3:12-13). Standing faithfully for the sake of the gospel, then, requires much courage and grace.

Marvel in a Sovereign God

Marveling in a sovereign God involves maintaining an eternal perspective. The Supreme Court decision did not take God by surprise. Christ is still on the throne. The psalmist acknowledges God's sovereign control over all things, even in light of a generation which appears to be dominated by wickedness:

> *"If the foundations are destroyed, what can the righteous do?"*
> *The LORD is in his holy temple; the LORD'S throne is in heaven; his eyes see, his eyelids test the children of man. The LORD tests the righteous, but his soul hates the wicked and the one who loves violence. Let him rain coals on the wicked; fire and sulfur and a scorching wind shall be the portion of their cup. For the LORD is righteous; he loves righteous deeds; the upright shall behold his face (Ps. 11:3-7).*

Jonathan Edwards never shrank back from declaring the full force of God's sovereignty. This God delights to display his justice and will vindicate the godly and unveil his wrath against the unrighteous:

---

[176] *Here We Stand: An Evangelical Declaration on Marriage,* June 2015.

At the day of judgment there will be the most glorious display of the justice of God that ever was made. Then God will appear to be entirely righteous toward everyone; the justice of all his moral government will be removed; the conscience of every man shall be satisfied; the blasphemies of the ungodly will be forever put to silence, and argument will be given for the saints and angels to praise God for ever. [177]

When the smoke clears, we realize the Supreme Court decision is not about civil rights or constitutional law. For the Christian, it has everything to do with a set of opposing world views. Scripture says, "Therefore God gave them up in the lusts of their hearts to impurity, to the dishonoring of their bodies among themselves, because they exchanged the truth about God for a lie and worshiped and served the creature rather than the Creator, who is blessed forever! Amen" (Rom. 1:24-25). It is in the midst of such a climate that we are called to serve God and faithfully live the Christian life.

Two days after the Supreme Court decision, John MacArthur wrote a letter to the alumni of the Master's Seminary. One section of the letter stands out: "Marriage is not the ultimate battleground, and our enemies are not the men and women who seek to destroy it (2 Cor. 10:4). The battleground is the gospel. Be careful not to replace patience, love, and prayer with bitterness, hatred, and politics."[178]

MacArthur is spot on. Indeed, the battleground is the gospel. Joe Thorn reminds us, "… It is important that you meditate on the gospel … You must learn, relearn, and remember your Savior's love and sacrifice for the wicked, the rebellious, the black-hearted - for people like you. And when you see the Holy One's sacrificial love for you, you not only see what love looks like, but also you find strength and power to love like him."[179]

Our task, then, is to lovingly and firmly engage with people in the postmodern milieu. "Conformity, not distinctiveness, is the way to a trouble-free life. So the more early Christian took their faith

---

[177] Jonathan Edwards, The Works of Jonathan Edwards, Vol. 2, *The Final Judgment on the World Judged Righteously by Jesus Christ* (Carlisle: Banner of Truth, 1834), 192.

[178] John MacArthur, *An Open Letter to The Master's Seminary Alumni* June 27, 2015.

[179] Joe Thorn, *Note to Self: The Discipline of Preaching to Yourself* (Wheaton: Crossway Books, 2011), 36.

seriously the more they were in danger of crowd reaction."[180] May we play an important part in strengthening foundations in an age in which truth is discounted and biblical morality is denied. May we stand faithfully in an age in which biblical standards are mocked and maligned. And may our love for the Savior propel us into the future by his grace and for his glory!

---

[180] Bruce Shelly, *Church History in Plain Language,* 42.